Do You Dot-Com?

A Field Guide to Understanding Life at an Internet Company

GUSTAV CARLSON

D1414078

AMACOM

American Management Association

New York • Atlanta • Boston • Chicago • Kansas City • San Francisco • Washington, D.C.
Brussels • Mexico City • Tokyo • Toronto

Special discounts on bulk quantities of AMACOM books are available to corporations, professional associations, and other organizations. For details, contact Special Sales Department, AMACOM, a division of American Management Association, 1601 Broadway, New York, NY 10019.
Tel.: 212-903-8316   Fax: 212-903-8083
Web site: www.amacombooks.org

This publication is designed to provide accurate and authoritative information in regard to the subject matter covered. It is sold with the understanding that the publisher is not engaged in rendering legal, accounting, or other professional service. If legal advice or other expert assistance is required, the services of a competent professional person should be sought.

Carlson, Gustav.
    Do you dot-com? : a field guide to understanding life at an Internet company / Gustav Carlson.
        p. cm.
    Includes index.
    ISBN 0-8144-7103-X (pbk.)
    1. Personnel management. 2. Electronic commerce—Management. I. Title.
HF5549 .C2935 2001
650.1—dc21   2001018864

Printing number

10 9 8 7 6 5 4 3 2 1

Contents

Preface

Inspiration can come in many forms: as a sign from above, in a familiar tune, with a lover's touch. And it usually comes when least expected. That's been my experience, anyway.

It was no different with *Do You Dot-Com?* On my first day working in the Internet economy, I picked up the company's internal telephone directory (they had it in hard copy form for old economy types like me) and looked for the number of Brian Scott, a technology person who would help me set up my computer. Without thinking, I flipped through the book, stopping two-thirds of the way through to roughly where the S section would be. It wasn't there. I looked more closely. The S section listed the following: Sally Brown, Samuel Young, Sandra Kahn. I scratched my head. What were Brown, Young, and Kahn doing in the S section? It took me a long, old-economy minute to figure it out. I looked again. Scarlett Parker, Sergio Rodriguez, Sylvia Orloski, all in the S's. I flipped quickly to the B section to prove my hunch. Yep, there was Brian Scott, in the B's—for Brian, of course. Indeed, the entire telephone directory was set up with given names (or Christian names, if you are truly ancient) listed first, and surnames second.

Aaron Zabar was at the front. Zachary Aardvark was at the back.

It was a remarkable discovery, I thought. How disturbingly familiar, to list people by their first names. And for someone like me, how utterly backward. I mean, I was raised on telephone books that listed people surname-first. In school, attendance and test scores were recorded and reported alphabetically, by surname, A to Z. The shrinks, of course, labeled this "alphabetical abuse" and claimed that it discriminated against kids whose names started with letters near the end of the alphabet. Those with names that started with Z were destined to become serial killers because they had to wait a couple of minutes longer to learn if they passed their second grade phonics test. (And that was the start of the disenfranchisement of every person in America.) But that was the way it was, for better or worse. A to L were overachievers who had a real shot at the White House or business success. M to Z were destined to be child molesters and realtors.

The trend continued in my business career. Recognition, good or bad, was delivered by surname. "Nice job, Carlson." Or more typically, "Carlson, you idiot. What the hell were you thinking?" Even in casual business conversation, it was surnames only. "Let Carlson do it," or "Hey, Carlson, come here a minute. We've got an assignment for you." Like in the military. Can you imagine a commander disciplining an underling using a first name? "I can't hear you, Adrian." Or inspiring his troops to go over the hill into a wall of oncoming bullets? "O.K. Ralph and Phil and Chucky, I need you to get in there and fight, fight, fight," instead of "Niedermeier, Blutarski, Wormer, get your asses in gear and take that f—ing hill." Hard to make that leap of faith, isn't it? Yes, in my day, which was not all that long ago, the use of given names was usually reserved for friends and family. They were not widely used in business, except in the most intimate or extraordinary circumstances. But more about that later.

To say the least, the dot-com phone book surprised me. It made me laugh, at first. But on reflection, it made me realize that there were apparently a whole lot of people for whom this made sense. A whole lot of people who wanted to be known, acknowledged, listed, addressed, and even reprimanded as Jim or Joan or Sid or Sally. Of course, I should not have been surprised. A combination of time compression and celebrity obsession had created a popular culture in which people were known by one name and only one name: Cher, Sting, Madonna, Bubba, Fridge. With less time on our hands, and the belief that to be known by only one name is a sign of importance, this trend was inevitable. And this phone book, I thought was the intermediate step—between the anonymity of the hierarchical old world and the celebrity of the new.

At that moment, as I fumbled through the book and realized that Brian Scott was listed under the B's and not the S's, I found inspiration. It was a little bit curiosity, a little bit fear and a lot of bemusement, frosted with a growing acknowledgment that somewhere deeper down was a story to be told. I wasn't sure at that point what the story was. But I was sure that somewhere between my view of the world and the telephone book author's view of the world, there was something worth exploring.

To this day, I still catch myself. If I'm in a hurry or don't stop and think first, I still flip to the wrong place in the company phone book. I look for Sam Adams in the front.

Adam Samuel nearer the back. And every time I do, I am reminded that it really is different in dot-com land. Sometimes for the better. Sometimes not. It all depends on how you see the world, and whether or not you're willing to accept the fact that there is always another view.

Acknowledgments

The most important contributors to this book don't even know they helped out. They are the characters I have met during my careers in the old economy (the people who taught me all the strict rules of engagement in business) and the new economy (the people who taught me how to break those rules). Without them and their wildly contrasting and often conflicting views of life in corporate America, there would no stories to tell.

There are some people, however, who stand out. Among them, my friend Mary Ellen Keating, who introduced me to life in the dot-com world and gave me the opportunity to become a part of it, and my editors, Ellen Kadin and Jim Bessent, who believed in the project through thick and thin. To them and everyone else who supported and tolerated me, many thanks.

> To my Mother,
> who taught me that life is much better
> on the lighter side.

Introduction

S o, you're intrigued by this dot-com thing? For years, you've been clawing your way up the "old-economy" corporate ladder, putting up with hierarchy and matrix management schemes, suffering idiot colleagues and abusive bosses. You've done what you've been told, put in long hours, bitten your tongue instead of speaking your mind. You've genuflected, ruminated. Sometimes, you've outright begged. All in the name of the middle manager's Holy Grail—a 4 percent annual raise.

You see the dot-com world as a land of opportunity. It is raw, dynamic, primal. Companies come and go. People come and go. It's like the Wild West. The Klondike. *Survivor*, with cell phones. Las Vegas, before the makeover.

You saw your neighbor's kid, a year out of college, sell his start-up, Snot.com, to some media conglomerate for enough cash to buy his own Gulfstream V. The plane, he tells you while you take a break from mowing your own lawn in the midday sun, is way better than its smaller sister, the G-IV. "I mean, Dude, I can Razor-scooter down the aisle without bruising the pumpkin."

— ◆ —

I thought casual dress meant a blue blazer and a shirt without French cuffs.

— ◆ —

Hate him. Admire him. But if you intend to emulate him, beware. The dot-com world is not for everyone, especially not for traditionally trained managers who are comfortable in the structured, striated world of Corporate America. Everything that made the Internet economy so successful in the first place is about breaking the rules. Doing things differently. Laughing in the face of convention.

If you've already made the move to dot-comland—or if you are a native—you know what I'm talking about. But believe it or not, you don't know everything, even if at age twenty-six your net worth is more than Canada's GDP for the entire 1990s. You could learn a thing or two from that dorky suit who used to work at Pepsico or Mastercard or General Motors. In fact, right now you might be wishing that suit had been around when it became clear that the most exciting feature of your dot-com company's business model was its ability to burn cash. That is, if you still have a company.

And if you work at a traditional company in the "offline" world—a so-called old-economy company—well, you've got problems of your own. You've probably watched the revolving door spin as your best managers trampled each other to hitch rides on the Internet safari to Silicon Valley or Silicon Alley. How do you keep them? How do you attract new ones? How do you get hip, cool? How do you become more "dot-com" without falling into the pitfalls that have sent so many Internet companies crashing and burning?

Well, you've come to the right place for the answers that no analyst—investment, industry, or psycho—can answer. A couple of years ago, I made the jump from the old economy to the new. Traditionally trained by some of America's stuffiest corporations, I believed in the credo "a place for everything and everything in its place." I obeyed my bosses, even if I hated them. I was grateful to have a job and a regular paycheck. I worried about asking for a raise. I considered leftover sandwiches from the boardroom to be a perk. I thought casual dress meant a blue blazer and a shirt without French cuffs.

Yet I found myself dazzled by the ballyhoo of the Internet. Maybe I should have listened to the alarm bells in my head during my first job interview at a dot-com. The company's offices were in a converted warehouse in New York City. As I was led from the reception area to a senior manager's office, I marveled at the cavernous open ceiling, with ductwork and wiring crisscrossing in a jumble.

"When will the construction be finished?" I chirped observantly to my escort, pointing to the mess overhead.

She stopped and scowled. "It was designed that way. By a famous architect. Industrial minimalism. Ever heard of it?"

— ◆ —

Be real.

Be yourself.

Be afraid.

— ◆ —

I hadn't, but I nodded my head anyway. I had learned Lesson One: If you're used to a workplace with things like walls and ceilings and doors, get over it. In dot-comland, it's all about bare concrete, exposed brick, open ceilings, and Jetson-style furniture that is so stylishly hip that it is comfortable for only those who weigh less than the federal government's guideline for their height.

See how frightening this is? And how unprepared you are? They didn't teach you this stuff at business school. And this is only the beginning.

If you want to turn back now, it's O.K. Everyone will understand. But if you're determined to go ahead, it's time to get serious. Let's start by finding out what you're made of. How close you are to being dot-com. Or, probably more to the point, how far away you are. And how much work you have to do to close the gap.

Take the following test. Don't cheat. Cheating is so "old economy." Be real. Be yourself. Be afraid.

As a child, I_____.

A. Obeyed my parents

B. Rebelled, but never got caught

C. Went to prison instead of high school

D. I am still a child

I have seen the CEO of my company _____.

A. Never

B. Only in our television commercials

C. Once, in an elevator, but he was distracted by the floor numbers lighting up and didn't really notice me

D. Every day at the combination boardroom/ basketball court

I have had ____ jobs since I graduated ____ ago.

A. One, twenty years

B. Three, ten years

C. Five, five years

D. Eight, fifteen minutes

I left my last job because

_____.

A. My boss was a jerk

B. I was a jerk

C. It was time for a change

D. Camp counselors can't work past eighteen

If my boss yells at me, I

_____.

A. Ask for forgiveness and promise to do a better job next time

B. File a complaint with OSHA

C. Cry

D. I don't have a boss, I have a "thought partner"

I joined my current company because it has

_____.

A. Opportunity for advancement

B. A learning environment

C. Subsidized lunches

D. An on-site climbing wall

If I drop a glass and it breaks, and I'm asked what happened, I say _____.

A. I was clumsy. I must be more careful next time.

B. It was an accident.

C. Adrian did it.

D. It was broken when I got here.

Twenty years ago, I was

_____.

A. In graduate school

B. In college

C. In high school

D. In vitro

Twenty years from now, I will be

_____.

A. Dead

B. CEO

C. Vested

D. In the Cayman Islands

Joe DiMaggio is best known as

_____.

A. The Yankee Clipper

B. Mr. Marilyn Monroe

C. Mr. Coffee

D. The director of *The Sopranos*

I liked Ringo Starr best _____.

A. As a Beatle

B. In his All-Star Revue Band

C. In *Poseidon Adventure*

D. In Charles Schwab ads

My hero is _____.

A. Jack Welch, Jr.

B. Bill Gates

C. Hillary Clinton

D. Spiderman

My work hours are _____.

A. 9 to 5

B. 8:30 to 5:30

C. 7 to 6

D. Whenever

When I stay late at work, I get _____.

A. Fulfillment and meaning

B. Time and a half

C. Indigestion

D. Stoked

When I see my boss in the morning, my usual greeting is _____.

A. "Good morning, Ms. Parker."

B. "Hi, Allison."

C. "Love your suit!"

D. Unintelligible.

When I get tired at work, I go _____.

A. For coffee

B. For a walk around the block

C. For a cigarette

D. To the nap room

I make business deals _____.

A. On the golf course

B. At dinner

C. On my cell phone

D. In the nap room

To me, "multitasking" is when I _____.

A. Walk and chew gum at the same time

B. Sit and chew gum at the same time

C. Talk and make sense at the same time

D. Walk, chew gum, work on my laptop, talk on the telephone, listen to my Walkman, watch television, check stock prices on my Palm Pilot, check e-mail on my Blackberry, at the same time

My favorite color is _____.

A. Black

B. Black

C. Black

D. Black

(For men): I shop for work clothes at _____.

A. Brooks Brothers

B. The Gap/Banana Republic

C. Kmart

D. Bang Bang

(For women): I shop for work clothes at _____.

A. Chanel

B. Ann Taylor

C. T.J. Maxx

D. Bang Bang

I wear pajamas _____.

A. To bed

B. To meetings

C. To dinner out

D. All of the above

My hair color is

_____.

A. Blond/brunette

B. Red

C. Other primary color (please specify)

D. I have no hair.

When I want to communicate with my colleagues about an important business initiative, I meet them_____.

A. At the water cooler

B. In a meeting room

C. In a chat room

D. At Starbucks

The most important program on my computer is_____.

A. Solitaire

B. Minesweeper

C. Pinball

D. Napster

My main source for news and current events is _____.

A. *The Wall Street Journal*

B. CNN

C. *People*

D. Vault.com

At their current value, my stock options will buy _____.

A. A four-bedroom house

B. A forty-foot sailboat

C. A Caribbean vacation

D. A Paul Anka eight-track tape

Don't panic if you didn't answer all of these questions. They're designed to be difficult. And did you notice the trick questions? Like the one about heroes? If you're over forty and answered "Spiderman," you get a bonus point because it's clear you haven't lost the ability to suspend disbelief. That ability will do you well in the dot-com world.

Or the question about multitasking? If you're under thirty and your answer was "Talking and making sense at the same time," you get a bonus point, too. That kind of talent is rare, and in great demand.

And how about the one about hair color? I imagine a lot of you over forty and under thirty chose "I have no hair," but probably for very different reasons. You see, there is common ground here, after all.

(And by the way, Ringo Starr wasn't in *The Poseidon Adventure*, but Ernest Borgnine was. And if you knew that, stop reading now and go back to your job at the insurance company.)

Now let's look at how you scored, and what those scores mean. The answers may save you a lot of embarrassment and humiliation. Believe me, I wish someone had given me this test before I made the jump.

Corporate Toady

If you answered A to most of these questions, you have to think twice about the dot-com world, or at least be prepared to go through some major behavior modification. Like I did. It is clear that your psyche is trussed up tighter than a Thanksgiving turkey. You love authority. You love hierarchy. You buy your boss gifts for every major occasion, including Arbor Day. You stay late at the office not because you have work to do, but because you hope that someone may notice your dedication and recommend you for a promotion.

Your view of discipline is that when necessary, it should be administered liberally and often—and you want to be first in line. You truly believe that there is a fine line between pleasure and pain, and you cross that line many times a day. You voted for Ronald Reagan. Your idea of risk taking is getting sprinkles on your vanilla ice cream. You love interoffice memos and tassled loafers. You are positively Jurassic. You are a tight-ass.

As you will learn throughout this book, you Corporate Toady types out there have the most adjusting to do in the dot-com world. It is a big leap. From conformity to randomness. From structure to chaos. From Streisand to Slash. It's not that you don't have the ability to do the work; it's that the environment may require so much adjustment that you simply can't concentrate enough to do it.

Pop quiz: Would it bother you if a colleague brought his dog to a business meeting? Of course it would. But what if the meeting and the dog were in the park, under that big leafy tree, right near the duck pond? And what if the reason for the meeting being there is that it is a beautiful summer day, too nice a day to be inside? If you're wondering what crackpot would have a business meeting in any place other than a meeting room, you fail the quiz. Stay put. Or be prepared to have a complete personality makeover, whichever is easier for you.

Closet Creative

If you answered B to most of these questions, well, at least you have enough flexibility to warrant a closer look at dot-com. And you won't need electroshock treatments to prepare yourself. You are still a slave to the old-world hierarchy, but you don't enjoy the structure as much as your Corporate Toady counterparts. You respect your boss, but in company with close friends, you admit she's a weasel. You still fear authority, but once in a while you charge a personal lunch with a friend back to the company. You are an undecided voter, maybe even a Republican-turned-Democrat. Once in a while, you'll try something exotic, like shark fin soup or Rollerblading. You want to succeed, to impress your parents, your family, or your friends, but you want some personal fulfillment, too. You have subscriptions to the *Economist* and *Self*. Once, you went on a bike trip with a friend through Chile. It is still the most interesting thing you've ever done.

You Closet Creatives can be swayed by dot-com, but it will take some convincing. You are attracted by the creative, organic nature that fosters fulfillment as well as money. But it's still pretty scary. A jump will mean cutting the umbilical cord for good, crawling out of the cocoon.

Pop quiz: Your company offers you free yoga classes during work hours. What do you do? You are tempted, because it's the kind of thing that appeals to you. But you feel guilty. Self-conscious. "Should I really be doing this at work?" Get over it, if you want to dot-com.

Desperately Seeking Something

These are the kind of people the Moonie's love to get at airports. If you answered C to most of these questions, you are ready to be convinced, persuaded, influenced. You are waiting to be led astray. You are impressionable and proud of it. You believed your friends when they said you were once abducted by aliens because you woke up after an all-night bender with strange red marks on your forehead. (If you could remember, you would know that the marks matched up perfectly with the handles on the refrigerator door in your kitchen.) You have a healthy distrust of authority, especially your boss, and not much respect for hierarchy. You liked ABBA, until the Yuppies rediscovered them.

The dot-com world tickles your curiosity. It speaks to the rebel in you, even though the most rebellious thing you've ever done is streak through your own backyard at three in the morning. You just need a little push, and not much attitude adjustment.

Pop quiz: Your company's distribution center is running short of people on the busiest night of the holiday shopping season and your boss asks you to give a hand packing boxes. What do you do? Unlike the Corporate Toady, who would never think of stooping so low as to do manual labor, or the Closet Creative, who knows it's the right thing to do but isn't sure if she should do it, you say, "Cool. I'll pitch in." Dot-com life is working its way into your consciousness. It may actually already be there. It just needs to be liberated.

Dot-Com Dynamo

If you answered D to most questions, you are at a dot-com already or you should be. You can write HTML code in your sleep. You skateboard to work in your pajama bottoms. You have a parrot named Roxanne who knows how to work your Palm Pilot. You have explored a surgical procedure that would replace your right hand with a mouse.

To you, authority doesn't simply suck; it is irrelevant. Hierarchy is left over from the days of the monarchy. The only divine right these days is the right of everyone to surf the net without constriction or consequence. You think hacking is an art form, not a crime. You wear nothing but black, and think Limp Bizkit are prophets. You have a tattoo of the yin and yang somewhere on your body, and at least one piercing. Sometimes, you become so involved with your job you forget to eat lunch.

Pop quiz: Your company's stock price is plummeting and you are asked to cut back on costs. What do you do? You change the voice mail on your office phone to say: "Don't bug me. But if you want to grab a latte at Starbucks, I'm at the Foosball table in Reception." You are hip. You are cool. You are dot-com.

I hate to break this to you, Buzz. As you will learn in the following pages, there is something that is quickly replacing hip in the Internet world. It's called accountability. It's something a lot of early dot-com companies didn't have. And you know where they went. Now I'm not suggesting that accountability is all about being a Corporate Toady tight-ass. But somewhere in between strict structure and creative abandon lies the secret to the next generation of dot-coms. You'll just have to all get along.

If you still haven't given up on the dot-com dream, I urge you to read on. You won't learn this stuff anywhere else. Not in the job interview. Not in the business model. Not in the investment analysts' reports about the dot-com sector. And that MBA you got? It won't help you understand this, either. All I can hope is that some old-economy company helped you pay for it.

Before we go on, I will warn you again. Dot-comland is not for everyone. It has produced a big heap of casualties of all ages and backgrounds. The only common thread is that they all wanted to roll the dice to be part of the most exciting age in business since, well, probably the Industrial Revolution.

And for those of you who think the dot-com thing is a fad, consider this. When was the last time you heard someone say, "You know, I've tried e-mail, but I don't like it? I think I'll go back to writing letters." The Internet is here to stay, and as the market grows, so will the demand for talented people of all stripes and from all backgrounds.

So come on. You can dot-com, too. Hell, I did. Or at least I'm trying. Good luck.

chapter one

On Authority

I have a healthy respect for authority. It is based on equal parts fear and necessity. It works like this: I fear that if I tick off the person whose signature appears on my paycheck, I will not make the money necessary to live my life. Pretty basic, primal motivation. It has worked well for me for more than twenty years of my work life. So why change now?

As all you Corporate Toadies will agree, that kind of respect for authority is what it's all about. But as the Dotcom Dynamos will tell you, that is simply the most horrible way imaginable to live your life.

Who's right? Consider this. Take an aging executive, his ingenue girlfriend, and his long-suffering wife living a life of denial, and what have you got? If you answered an average day in the White House for our forty-second Pres-

ident, you're close—but no . . . well, you know how that
old joke ends. Change the names, move the scandal to New
York, but keep the dynamics the same, and you've got what
the *New York Post* called "The Kinky Tycoon" scandal.

The players: A prominent seventy-year-old investment
banker, his young fashion model trophy, and his wife of
many years pacing the floors of their Connecticut mansion
wondering why, at such a late stage in his career, he has to
work such long hours.

— ◆ —

Why tell the CEO?

He'd just get mad.

— ◆ —

The bombshell: Girlfriend finds out that Sugar Daddy is
cheating on her with another model and slaps him with a
multimillion dollar lawsuit, claiming damages for "promises
broken." The public airing of laundry can only make things
worse for the already unhappily wedded couple.

Oh, and there's one more thing you've got in this little
circus: a hot potato for the person who has to tell the head
of the Wall Street firm that employs the philandering
senior that the publicity surrounding the scandal will be
bad, very bad. That person, if you haven't guessed already,
would be me.

It happened in the summer of 1998, while I was working on Wall Street. The scandal was real, and it was ugly.
The New York City tabloids had the story, plus they had

photos of the randy banker, the sultry siren, and the humiliated wife, weeping on the front forty of the expansive estate that would soon be hers. I had the choice job of letting the chairman know that the firm's name would be all over the headlines the next day.

I also had the sympathy of my colleagues. No one likes to have to tell the boss bad news. Especially a boss this big and news this bad. To disappoint an authority figure is no fun for a traditionally trained manager, even if the disappointment is not of your making. But that's the kind of responsibility that falls to you as you climb the ladder of corporate accountability. It is what you have been trained for all of your career. Like the pilot, who for years studied and practiced and flew in war games, and finally finds himself in the middle of a dogfight at 30,000 feet over the Pacific with a real live bogey. I could hear the words in my ear: "This is not a drill."

I tried to think of ways to make the situation more palatable to Mr. Big. To low-key it. To sugarcoat it. It was simply a lover's quarrel, I could say. No one will pay attention. Besides, who reads the tabloids, anyway? I mean, who that really matters? Who was I kidding? Sex, money, power, infidelity, beauty, betrayal. This was a miniseries waiting to happen. There was no way I could make this into a silk purse, publicitywise. As good old-economy managers say when they can't wriggle their way out of a problem, "It is what it is." I had to suck it up and bear the bad news. It was my job. It was my duty. I was prepared to die for my company.

Fast-forward to the dot-com world. I was doing some consulting work for a dot-com, and while trying to get access to its Web site one morning, I was foiled, time and time again. I could not get in and received a series of error messages on my computer screen. I called the head of technology.

"Is the site down?" I asked.

"What do you mean?"

"I mean is the site down? I've tried a dozen times and I can't get in."

"Oh, that," he replied. "Yep. It's down."

I asked him for how long, and he replied about twelve hours.

"Did you tell anyone?" I asked.

"Like who?"

"Like the CEO, the COO, the CFO?"

"Why would I tell them? They'd just get mad."

I stopped short. Why would he tell the people in charge about a potentially devastating situation for the company that would be discovered eventually by someone? "They'd just get mad." Of course. Interesting logic. I thought about the sex scandal. Would I have been in more trouble with the big boss by telling him or by not telling him? Should I have simply let him find out about it in the paper? After all, it wasn't my fault.

My training told me that the former was the only proper way to go, and that's how I went. (For those of you who are wondering how the Wall Street biggie took the news of the aging Lothario in his employ and the impending firestorm of bad publicity, his answer was simple and typically old economy: "It is what it is.")

Frankly, I had never considered the alternative of not telling my boss the bad news. Naive? Maybe. Respectful? Certainly. Old economy? Absolutely. But the alternative was obviously the preferred choice in the dot-com world. I wondered how much stuff went on at a dot-com that no one bothered to share with those in charge. It was clear that the answer was lots. But it wasn't because the dot-comers were inherently deceitful. They simply had a different view of authority, and their responsibility to it.

And therein lies the rub. Authority is a funny thing. Either you love it or you hate it. Sort of like Yoko Ono's singing. Or brussels sprouts. To me, they're the same horrible experience. Just different orifices.

Traditional managers are trained to respect authority. In fact, the old economy was built on and still thrives on authority. Yes, sir. No, sir. That report will be on your desk by nine, sir.

If you are a Corporate Toady, you are probably a decent old-economy manager. You do what you're told. You deliver on time and on budget, the same way you used to sit up straight and eat all your vegetables. You are motivated by the need for approval, fearful of screwing up and, in the process, losing the respect of those in the higher ranks. You live for the raise, or the year-end bonus. They are the cheese at the end of the maze. The biscuits doled out to you every time you press the correct button.

Now don't get me wrong. All these are admirable qualities. They have been the backbone of Corporate America for years. This country's suburbs are filled with examples of those who do this with skill and aplomb, all mowing their own lawns, washing their own cars, and faithfully kissing their bosses' asses five days a week.

But if you want to work in the dot-com world, unpucker. You've got some loosening up to do.

On the Internet, authority is a foreign concept. There is nowhere near as much sucking up as in the old economy. That's because the entire Internet is built upon the idea of "community." Freedom of expression and exchange. An electronic mosh pit of ideas, information, and insight, churning around in cyberspace, with technology allowing the whole process to defy conventional limits. A beautiful thing. Spiritual, natural, untarnished by rules and regulations.

Why do you think the hackers who have crippled e-commerce sites in the past did what they did? It wasn't usually for money. There are no rewards for Most Valuable Hacker. In fact, the opposite is true. The risks of prosecution are very high. The FBI and most big-city police forces now have special Internet crime divisions that specialize in hacking. Yet they continue to fiddle with the innards of commercial sites as a way of protesting the commercialization of the medium. The imposition of limits. The encroachment of capitalism onto what has been in essence a vehicle of democratization.

The average hacker probably went to prison instead of high school. Make a note of this in your career development notebook. Up the river is not the same as up the ladder.

In fact, it is this "rebel with a mouse" shtick that has helped hackers to become the underground heroes of many in the dot-com world. Revolutionaries. Freedom fighters.

How much are they revered? In 1999, a hacker broke into a number of big e-commerce Web sites and tried to extort money from the companies that ran them. True to form for a hacker, he didn't seek a lot of money—$100,000 or so, far less than he could have squeezed from companies with combined sales in the billions. The reign of cyber-terror was front-page news in the *New York Times* and other media outlets. The FBI and police forces across the country followed leads and tips and worked their contacts to the bone.

But the big break came on a fluke. A woman went into a video arcade somewhere in the Midwest to get change for a dollar to buy a coffee. While she was waiting for the clerk to make change, she overheard a group of teenagers talking about a computer hacker whom one of them knew. They were raving about how great he was, how cool he was, how he was sticking up places like Amazon.com and eToys. To these kids, the hacker was a combination Robin Hood and Arnold Schwarzenegger, or Joan of Arc and Rambo.

The woman was on the ball. She called the police, who questioned the teens, who led them to the hacker. And the story ended happily, for the companies.

But here's a secret. What the hackers are doing isn't that new. Only their methods have changed. We've seen these folks before—in the 1960s. Back then, they got together in places like Haight-Ashbury and Isla Vista and carried signs that read "Ban the Bomb" and "Hell no, we won't go." Sometimes, they destroyed things, like Bank of America branches. Stuff like that. But their message was the same: Screw Authority.

Sometimes, hackers' efforts have been less destructive, unless of course you're Microsoft or the recorded music industry. Hackers can be creative and constructive. Look at the success of Linux, MP3, Napster, and Gnutella. Powerful, pervasive, but vehicles of protest, nonetheless. These grew organically and were expanded without any sort of

— ◆ —

Is an employee

entitled to talk

to the CEO?

— ◆ —

corporate process basically by a group of independent hackers around the globe unified by one guiding principal: making the Internet the domain of everyone. To almost everyone's amazement, Linux has actually gained enough market share to make mighty Microsoft sweat, and Napster became so powerful that the only way for the music moguls to fight it was to buy it, which they did.

That same sentiment of rebellion has crept into the dot-com companies. Why? Because in the early stages of the dot-com, it was the technology experts who drove the growth. They were the ones who figured out how to put all the pieces together. They configured the systems, wrote the code, and made the Web sites fun, functional, and friendly. And although the marketing people eventually moved into positions of power, followed by the finance people who came along to spoil the party, the Internet is still and always will be the techies' domain. And, therefore, authority will always be viewed with a certain amount of suspicion, and those in positions of authority will be subject to derision.

You want it in simpler terms? Think about that time your parents came home early from vacation and you were having a party at the house for 300 of your closest friends. Nuff said.

If you think I'm being overly dramatic about the rebel conscious of the Internet, consider this:

One day, not long after I had arrived in the dot-com world, I got a panicked call from a young employee in Web site production. She was all of twenty-three years old, and her entry-level position was her first out of college. She was green, brilliant, and enraged.

"I am really pissed off," she said. "I e-mailed the CEO about my project this morning and I haven't heard back yet. I need you to let him know I want to talk to him as soon as possible."

My response was typical of an old-economy meanie: "What are you doing e-mailing the CEO, anyway?" And while I didn't say it aloud, I was also thinking, "and what makes you think the seniormost executive in the company cares what you think, anyway?"

I mean, where I come from, people at all levels, but especially those in steerage, go out of their way to avoid any and all contact with senior management. Am I right about this?

That's why they have separate bathrooms. So you don't have to talk to them, and they don't have to talk to you. It's a perfect setup.

But this employee didn't think so. It was clear that I was the only one in the conversation who knew the Rules of Engagement for senior management. Or, more precisely, I was the only one who knew that such rules existed.

The exchange raised an interesting point. Was the employee entitled to talk to the CEO? Why not? In fact, do you think this kind of empowerment has any relationship to the ability of Internet companies to get products from concept to market in a fraction of the time it takes their old-economy counterparts to do so? Duh.

I had heard someone say once that if you can't e-mail your CEO, you don't have a technology problem; you have a culture problem. That day, I understood what that meant.

So, what does this have to do with you? Well, it means that if you are a Corporate Toady or a Closet Creative, you probably would have been a lousy hacker. And you probably think people who use Napster are no better than bikers. You have no purpose. No passion. No healthy disrespect for anything, except maybe yourself. Authority is king, no matter what. And you may have trouble getting used to the dot-com world.

If you are Desperately Seeking Something, you're on the right track. Because the Internet world is filled with rebels, including reluctant ones. But the smart ones have learned to harness their rebellious energy for more constructive purposes. Or maybe more correctly, the market has taught the rebels that if you blow all your money on fancy Web sites and cool advertising and leave nothing for building the systems needed to deliver products to your customers, you will go out of business. It's sort of a basic rule of business, online and off: "If you build it, they may come, but if you don't keep your promise, they won't come back." If you break this rule, you will most likely be a rebel without a job.

If you are a Dot-Com Dynamo, no matter what your age, you've learned that defying authority, or ignoring it, is what the Internet is all about. Acting like children actually has its benefits. Why? Because children learn. In fact, they like to learn. They're not afraid to try, even if it means falling down. They're not self-conscious about it. They know what they don't know, which is just about everything. Best of all, they're not constrained by convention. Old habits don't die hard with children because there are no old habits.

But equally important, children have a very strong sense of wonder. And you need a healthy dose of wonder to understand the Internet world. It is really too big a concept for most people to understand. Like why a plane flies. Or why the sky is blue. Or why David Hasselhoff is a star.

Hard to believe, isn't it? Not the Hasselhoff thing. I mean it's hard to believe that the world is connected by this incredible technology. You have to suspend disbelief a little bit. You have to be a little rebellious in the way you think, and in the way you act. It's not that bad, even if it goes against your training.

So if you're a Corporate Toady or a Closet Creative, go ahead, try it. Stay up later than usual on a weeknight. Have that extra scoop of ice cream. Admit to the world that you have the collected works of the Captain and Tenille, including a signed poster.

Feels good, doesn't it? You're getting the hang of it. Next thing you know, you'll be sending the CEO of your company an e-mail, demanding a response about that project that's so important to you. And when he fires you, you're ready for a job at a dot-com.

chapter two

On Hierarchy

To get from my office to the chairman's office at my Wall Street company, I had to run the following gauntlet:

- Four card-access-only doors, with video surveillance cameras

- Three armed security guards

- Three secretaries (executive assistants)

- Twelve pieces of Impressionist art, only two of which I understood (though I would bet money that one of them was hung upside down)

To get from my first office in the dot-com world to the chairman's office, I ran this gauntlet:

- Fifty feet of floor, half-carpeted in amoeba-shaped pastel swatches, half-exposed raw concrete

- Four mousetraps

- A golden retriever named Alfie, owned by a secretary

- A cappucino machine

Things sure are different here in dot-com land. For the traditionally trained manager, all the usual reference points are gone. There are no trail markers, no notches in the

It's sort of like

Woodstock, but

with shareholders.

trees, no milestones. It's sort of like the *Blair Witch Project*, without the tents. The main point of commonality is that if there ever was a map, someone lost it. O.K., in recent times, you could simply look up to see the vultures circling to find out where all the dot-com executives had gone. But even in the best of times, Hänsel and Gretel would get lost here.

They also have a much different way of getting information through the pipeline in the dot-com world, mainly because there is no pipeline in the traditional sense. It is more of a cyber-mosh pit. Sort of Woodstock, but with shareholders. Here's what I mean.

There is something in the dot-com world called an "all-hands meeting." It is a peculiar ritual, part business meeting, part pep rally, part evangelical service. It is the product of old-economy thinking with an Internet spin. Think Little League, but with keyboards instead of bats.

It begins with a group of employees congregating in an open area. The more, the better. The goal, after all, is "all hands." Like on a ship that's in distress. Or a creepy date.

The casual, unstructured nature of the gathering is by design. Don't hem me in, it says. Yet you can tell the old-economy managers. They feel compelled to form some sort of order from the chaos. They can't help themselves. Moving about the crowd like sheepdogs, they herd the flock forward, barking and growling, nudging them ever so gently toward the center of attention.

The CEO appears like Phil Donahue (or in more contemporary terms, like Jerry Springer). He jumps up on a table, or a chair. He assumes a John Wayne stance, hands on hips. A gunslinger. He shouts stuff like, "Are we kickin' ass?" The crowd stirs. He continues: "Are we a hot site or what?" The voices of the congregation are raised in response: "Yeah." The CEO throws his arms wide and shouts heavenward: "Keep it up, everyone."

And then, head down, he whispers: "Any questions?"

But everyone's too busy to ask questions. Besides, only a few people know what to ask, and the CEO isn't going to

answer those tough ones anyway. Quickly, and with a flourish, he is gone. Strategy session over. Long live dot-com.

The crowd disperses, energized but somehow empty.
Like they've just watched a Steven Seagal movie. Or eaten
Chinese food. It looked good, tasted good, but their stom-
achs are already growling again. That really wasn't filling
at all.

If you're a Corporate Toady, stop shaking your head
in disgust. Don't feel so high and mighty, so far above
such juvenile attempts to generate excitement and good-
will inside a company. At least these people have seen
their CEO.

What everyone has to remember is that hierarchy, in
any form, complex or simple, is a product of authority—
the same way that the hockey pucks used in shinny games
on the frozen ponds in the Midwest are products of local
cattle. They both have value, but they're mostly just BS.
And your ability to see it, smell it, and avoid stepping in it
is directly related to your prospects for success in business,
no matter which economy you choose.

Hierarchy, as any good dot-comer will tell you, is the
Establishment's way of protecting themselves. It is a control mechanism. As long as there are layers and rules and
ladders to climb, and as long as they are on top, they are
protected. They can pour hot oil down from the ramparts
whenever the peasants revolt. But put these people in an
"all-hands" meeting at a dot-com and they would be like
the gazelles on the Discovery Channel: dinner.

The good news for all concerned is that hierarchy, in
the traditional sense, anyway, is pretty much a dirty word

in the dot-com world. This is not surprising in a universe where authority is held in contempt.

But that's also the bad news. Without hierarchy, who's in charge? Who has the big ideas? Who makes the decisions? At a lot of dot-com companies, the answer to each question is, or was: no one. The democratization of everything, including power, is fine in concept. But it's an awful way to run a business.

— ◆ —

Everything changed when someone said, "Hey, I bet we can make a buck out of this."

— ◆ —

Just ask the dot-coms that made the mistake early on of putting too much of their money into advertising and not enough into the processes of checks and balances that make a company work, particularly the back-end operations like distribution and fulfillment. Many of these companies hired senior executives who were marketing people, media hounds who spent more time appearing on CNBC and going to Internet conferences than they did running the operations, paying attention to detail, and setting up systems and processes that were essential to building a business. These talking heads and pretty faces fueled the hysteria surrounding the Internet, but in the end they did no one any favors. If they cashed out, they were lucky. If not, they're probably scrambling to find middle management jobs in the marketing departments of old-economy companies. In their wakes they left an Internet economy that is paying their debts, and retrofitting for accountability.

Now, the consultants will tell you that this hubbub about hierarchy and the new economy's discomfort with it all has to do with trends in society. That it is tied to the breakdown of the nuclear family, the collapse of family values. That because people no longer grow up in conventionally structured personal environments, they feel uncomfortable in structured professional environments. No one gave them orders, so they don't know how to take orders. No one set an example, so they don't even know what an example is. They don't know what loyalty means, so they lease their skills to companies until a better offer comes along. Their role models are spoiled, self-indulgent professional athletes and entertainers who report to no one but themselves. And they seem to be doing O.K. Basically, these experts will tell you that pretty much everyone in America today is in some way disenfranchised, and because of that hierarchies don't work.

Uh-huh. And the forty-second president of the United States did not have sexual relations with that woman, Monica Lewinsky. But it is not that complicated, no matter what your definition of "it" is. The point is that the dot-com business came into this world backward. It was a breech birth. And its approach to hierarchy, like its attitude to authority, reflects this rather inelegant entrance into the world of commerce.

The Internet didn't start as a pure business proposition. In fact, as we discussed in Chapter One, certain purists still rage against the commercialism of the Web. Despite Al Gore's claim of authorship and the military's early use of the network, the Internet has grown because it is a garden for everyday, average, run-of-the-mill techies. They planted it, cultivated it, nurtured it. Everyone contributed. Everyone extracted pleasure and value. Sort of like passing the dutchie. And as long as no one tried to hog it, bogey it, or sell it, there was no need to make or enforce rules. And therefore, no need for a process to do so.

— ◆ —

All matrix management meant was that I had to do everything in quadruplicate.

— ◆ —

That all changed when someone said, "Hey, this is pretty cool. I bet we can make a buck out of this thing." The commercial interests pushed, and the purists pushed back. This titanic struggle is still going on. That's why it has taken so long for hierarchies to be built in the dot-com world. And why the idea of process in an organic environment will always be an unholy alliance.

If the Internet had unfolded the other way, things probably would have been different. If someone had said, "I want to create a business that makes money, and I want to do it by setting up this global technology network that will allow me instant access to everyone with a computer, and

I'm going to develop a process by which this is imple-
mented," we probably wouldn't be having this discussion
right now. The Internet probably would have unfolded like
any old-economy market, and it probably would be only a
fraction as powerful and pervasive as it is today.

And I want all of you old-economy types who were just
about to start cheering in praise of process to think about
that. The Internet would not have been so revolutionary if
its creative power had been constrained by process in the
early going. The Internet was and still is all about the mul-
tidirectional flow of power through every blood vessel of
the Web, even down to the capillaries.

So forget all that junk you've been spoon-fed about how
power flows from the top down. Because if you have been
paying attention during your career, you'd know that in the
old economy in particular, power doesn't flow at all, up or
down. It collects at the top, like a clot, clouding judgment
and causing fits of flawed decision making in the upper-
most ranks, reminiscent of the French nobility.

Oh, they make you think that's not true. The management experts come up with these schemes with fancy
names, like "matrix management." It involves a complicated grid that lays functional capabilities over opera-
tional responsibilities, with geographical reach spread
over the top like frosting on the cake. The sell-in to
employees is that it actually fosters the flow of power to
all parts of the organization, and empowers everyone at
every level to make a difference.

I had a matrix management scheme laid on me one
day at an old-economy company. I felt like Gulliver in a

Lilliputian net. Instead of reporting to one person, I reported to four. I not only did my own work, just like before, but I also shouldered the administrative burden of keeping the flow of communications going through the matrix. All that really meant was that everything I did was in quadruplicate.

Some of America's biggest companies love matrix management. Even the technology companies, which are scratching their heads wondering why the dot-coms are eating their lunch. Maybe they should look a little more closely at how this process works, or rather, doesn't work.

In a matrix management system, if you're a manager in one division, and you want to communicate with, say, a vice president in another division, you cannot go as the crow flies. That's like the jester taking an important communiqué directly to the king.

No, you must go through a series of corporate food tasters who protect the vice president. You start by contacting your organizational equal in the division in question, who then takes the request up the tree to the higher branches. Up there, as we all know, the air gets pretty thin and the tails on the squirrels get pretty bushy. The response takes the reverse route. God help the vice president who responds directly to a lower-level person in another division. They would certainly revoke his executive bathroom privileges.

The process is not only cumbersome, but also unproductive. And it doesn't spread power at all. What it really does is tire everyone out, trying to figure out what channels are appropriate and then trying to navigate them. In the end, they have no energy, desire, or time to accumulate any power at all. In fact, they push power away, because they're too busy administering the organized confusion that is the matrix.

So there's all this discarded, unwanted power floating around out there, looking for a place to go for shelter. And guess who scoops it up, takes it inside where it's warm and dry, and gives it a good home? That's right. The real power continues to reside at the top. It's brilliant really, in an old-economy way. Problem is, the statue of the matrix will come tumbling down eventually, just like his did.

If you are a Corporate Toady, and you want to work in the dot-com world, you have to start weaning yourself of blind faith to strict hierarchy. You have no choice on this, because it is inconsistent with the mindset of the Internet. You must start to understand that while structure in the traditional sense has its value, it is not the be all and end all. It can be an impediment to growth—both for your company and for yourself. It inhibits the free flow of ideas, and, frankly, it perpetuates ideas of class and exclusion that are vestiges of different times and should have been discarded long ago. (And remember that denial is a river running smack through the middle of the old economy.) In the end, you must realize that structure means never having to say you're sorry. Indeed, if you're a senior manager, it sometimes means never having to say anything at all.

Closet Creatives will have less trouble with this transition. You are less dependent on a strict hierarchical system, though you still cling to it for security. Let go a little. Stick your head into that vice president's office without making an appointment. Say you had a great idea and it couldn't wait. It will feel good. And you will be amazed at how productive you can be if you aren't weighed down by the administrative burden of an old-economy hierarchy.

For you Desperately Seeking Somethings, be careful. The temptation here is to think that all hierarchy is bad. That restricting creative freedom through process and procedure is tantamount to clipping the wings of a dove. The recent lessons of the dot-com world clearly indicate that this is not true. You can't run around with wild abandon, expending time, energy, and resources randomly. You can't always get what you want, no matter what they tell you in television commercials. There is a reason that order is important. That limits are sometimes more important than chaos.

If you are a Dot-Com Dynamo who still has a job, you know now why it is important to find the middle ground between the gulag of the old economy and the outer space of the Internet. You've seen the amazing things that can be accomplished in an environment of pure freedom. But you've also seen the destruction that pure randomness can bring. Learn the lesson that in business, like in life, it's all about balance. Too much of one thing, even a good thing, can be a bad thing. Like eating a whole quart of ice cream at once. Sure it tastes great, but you're going to get a headache afterward.

What everyone needs to remember is that there is no rule that says senior management needs to be cloistered away in their executive suites, separated from their charges by security guards, bulletproof glass, and snarling secretaries. That authority is somehow diminished simply because senior managers have familiar relations with the troops, which sometimes includes a friendly game of hoops at lunch. That interoffice memos are somehow as effective as all-hands meetings.

Indeed, this is one of the best old-economy rules to break. Because good ideas can come from anywhere in the company. And it's a shame if the decision makers can't hear them through the thick oak doors of their corner offices.

chapter three
On Loyalty

When I decided to make the jump from the old economy to the new, what I made myself this promise: Get a big title. The big money, from what I had seen in the Internet world at the time, would take care of itself. O.K., so I was wrong. Didn't I say earlier that you could learn a lot from my mistakes? Do as I say, not as I do? I was sure I made that clear.

Anyway, early on, I thought, the title was the thing. It established your status in the pecking order, defined your identity, infused you with the appropriate amount of power. It was a bond with the company, a blood oath. If you grant me this title, I will repay you with loyalty, fealty. Sir Lancelot of dot-com.

For me a big title meant a step up, from vice president to senior vice president, or even executive vice president. Why not, I thought. I was coming into an environment where I had twenty years' more experience than 90 percent of the workforce. So what if I was a big fish in a pond of minnows. I was going to take this risk, and if it didn't work out, at least my resume would show that I had moved out to move up. I was upwardly mobile, professionally speaking.

I prepared to make my case to the recruiter. I would negotiate on money, but on title I would stand firm. I laid it out.

No one seemed to care what my title was. They didn't even care about their own.

"There are no senior vice presidents," she said. "Everyone's a vice president, I think. Everyone your age, anyway."

I haggled and balked and feigned lack of interest in the whole thing. I even made the case that the company would do better with an SVP or two, to lead, to set an example, to establish process and procedure.

"Sorry," she said. "No one really cares that much. It's not the same as you're used to."

I didn't believe her, but I took the job anyway. And two years later, I was still vice president. I hadn't moved up at all, nor had I moved down. But you know what, I seemed to be the only one who noticed. No one else seemed to care what my title was. They didn't seem to care about their own titles, either. The recruiter was right. But it's weird, don't you think? Spooky, even. What is wrong with these people?

Clearly, if a big title, an executive parking space, and a gold watch commemorating thirty years of service are important to you, stop right here. You are wasting your time even considering a life at a dot-com. Even if you get a big title, no one will pay any attention to it. Except maybe you. And if that's the case, you may be institutionalized for boasting loudly to yourself about your own status.

Not that I'm passing judgment on the relative importance of the trappings of executive life. When I was growing up, that's what work was all about. You got a job. You worked your way up the ladder, slowly but surely. You did menial tasks, kept your boss happy, paid your dues. And one day, if you didn't screw up too much or make too many enemies in high places, you let loose with this battle cry: "I made VP!" The company took care of you, and you repaid it with years of loyal service.

But not so fast, young hotshots, scoffing at the paternalism of the old corporate culture. If you think you can hop from job to job anymore in the dot-com world, you're out of step, too. Those days are pretty much over. Mainly because there are fewer places to which to hop. And less money to be made in the hopping. Mobility isn't what it used to be in the early days of the Internet, though it is still leaps and bounds ahead of your father's business world.

To find the happy medium in today's dot-com world, both sides have to understand the changes going on when it comes to loyalty and longevity in the era of the Internet.

Ten years ago, I attended a seminar held by a consulting company that specialized in workforce management. The theme was "Understanding the Attitudes of the New Worker: Lessons for Established Managers." What the title really meant was how fogies and snots can get along in a work environment without killing each other so their companies can make a little dough. It was an age-old issue, repackaged by consultants, and billed out at $1,000 a head. Nice work, if you can get it.

Most of us in the audience were cocky baby boomers, eager to learn how to manage the new breed of employees, who were members of Generation X. What we wanted most were tips on how to force these people to listen to what we said, because they seemed to have this idea that they didn't really need to listen to us at all. In fact, we got this sneaking suspicion that we were supposed to listen to them. Sound familiar?

What was interesting was that most of the discussion centered not on the relationship between the two sides but on how Generation X's views of work and career differ from our own, and from the generations before the baby boomers. Somewhere in that chasm lies some interesting insight into the differences between the dot-com world and traditional companies, as it applies to employers' relationships with employees—and employees' relationships with their employers.

Generation Xers, and those who have come along since then, we were told, are not slackers. To which almost everyone in the audience replied, "Prove it."

Indeed, we were told, they are actually far more self-directed and self-reliant than the boomers. They do not feel they have the collective strength that boomers have, and in fact they resent the boomers' amazing ability to consume and consume and consume—everything from material possessions to jobs—leaving them in the backwash of an economic jet stream.

— ◆ —

How value is created

and how the market views

it has changed.

— ◆ —

So they are making their own way. And they dislike or distrust or simply don't care about the institutions that their older colleagues have created as seats of power. They are mercenary. They are self-absorbed. And they are smart.

Smart because, whether they know it or not, their view of the business world was actually more in step with what was going on in the economy as a whole. As the economy moved away from industrial production and manufacturing and toward service-based companies, the nature of value— how it is created and how the market views it—changed, too. Value is no longer created by the machines owned by companies. It lies in the knowledge that employees bring with them to work every day. The problem is that intellectual property leaves the premises every day. And all the company can hope for is that it will show up for work the next day.

When people realized that this change was going on, their view of work changed. If I create the value, they concluded, indeed if I am the vessel in which value resides, I have the power. The power to choose where, for whom, and under what conditions I work. As long as I have the power to create value, I can go anywhere I want. And if where I am doesn't please me, or if another offer comes along that is better, I am under no obligation to stay. I will lease my talents to the highest bidder. And if they want to keep me, they will train me, compensate me, and make me comfortable. I will be a gun for hire, the Red Adair of the career world, a corporate gigolo.

This new realignment of loyalty—to oneself, rather than to a company—turned the goals and expectations of this new generation upside down. Why commit to a company for thirty years, laboring up the corporate ladder, so that one day you will be named regional vice president for sales and distribution? Your father may have wanted that on his tombstone, but will you? Not on your life.

Today's workers seek training and skills building, not executive parking spaces and gold watches at retirement. They want control of their own fate more than they want recognition. They want fulfillment before money. They want a workplace that energizes them, that makes them feel challenged and alive, not a stuffy rabbit warren full of middle managers in their cages, nibbling on the wood chips of bureaucracy.

The market has rewarded that thinking, penalizing industrial companies that had extensive physical plant resources and rewarding those that had intellectual potential. Why do you think concepts like knowledge management have become so important? And so difficult to make work?

We, the boomers, walked away from that seminar believing that, yes, indeed, there is life on Mars. And some of the Martians had come to work here, on earth, in our companies.

Control and fulfillment, instead of money and recognition? What kind of screwed-up group was this, anyway? That won't buy BMWs and beach houses in Bali and season tickets to the Yankees. These people will never amount to anything, we thought. Then along came the Internet. And our whole generation was overtaken in a few years.

The Internet was a perfect fit for this new mindset. It was organic, nonauthoritarian, nonhierarchical. Job fulfillment was top priority. Doing something meaningful was more important than doing something that was commercially successful. And in the Internet world, there were all sorts of ways for people to express their individuality.

And everything was new, so there were no preconceived ideas about the way things should be done. It was not a boomer institution at all. In fact, its very nature defied all that was about conformity and materialism and conspicuous consumption. There could not have been a more complementary medium for the new breed of worker. The planets aligned like never before, and there was magic, although the beauty of it all depended on which end of the wand you got.

Of course, things always get more complicated when there is money involved. Even the strongest-willed can be tempted. Every person has his price, and dot-com people are no exception.

The promise of the Internet as a commercial vehicle brought Wall Street to the dot-com world in a way that some say was like bringing the serpent to Eden. All of a sudden, the prospect of overnight millions provided another reason to job-hop. In fact, the Internet world, with its insane compensation packages and "sure thing" IPOs, encouraged it. If you were twenty-six and had had fewer than three or four jobs since graduation from college, you were a loser. Turnover at Internet companies was at levels so high they were unheard of in Corporate America. Yet for every person who walked out the door of an Internet company, there was another one walking in. They would stay a few months, learn a thing or two, then be gone.

I had a good friend who worked in the affiliate program at a dot-com company. I spoke with him one day about a joint project we were exploring, and then didn't speak with him for a few weeks. When we connected again, I learned that during those few weeks, he had left the company, had gone to another, had lived through its IPO, had cashed out his stock options, and had returned to the original company. I didn't even know he had been away. (Another update for your career notebook: You have to pay attention in the dot-com world. Stuff happens at lightning speed. Blink, and you've missed it.)

Another friend worked at five different dot-coms in a single year. And with each move she made, she increased her compensation by at least 20 percent. She also got a pocketful of stock options at each stop along the way and wisely cut deals on her departure that allowed her to cash at least a percentage of them, overriding the vesting requirements. I asked her what being in the revolving door was like.

It was like going to five different parties in one night. I can't really remember where they were, who was there, or what we did, but I know we had fun. And the next morning, I had a few bucks in my pocket and a few more saved. And I'm twenty-three.

Why is all this important to know? Well, lots of reasons. Although the hysteria of the Internet has died down, and although overnight millionaires are no longer the order of the day, the view of employment and career remains.

— ◆ —

You may not be invited to share herbal tea at break time.

— ◆ —

If you are an old-economy manager who hopes to be a manager in a dot-com, you have to compensate for this. You must be prepared to run a fluid organization, one that can flex to accommodate these attitudes. If your people want to telecommute (that's modern HR talk for goofing off at home), let them. If they want to break their workday up into three parts—10 to 2, 4 to 7, and 8 to 10—who cares, as long as they get their work done? If they want to bring their dogs to work, well, if you're not breaking any health codes, why not? These are not bad things. Remember, a happy employee is a productive employee.

Where you will run into trouble is when your people want to do something "cool" that doesn't have a hope in hell of making any money. Like a Web site that promotes "community," an ethereal, mystical concept that is one of the many bugaboos of the dot-com world. It will cost money to design, build, test, launch, maintain, and promote. It will be a beautiful thing. It will be an expression of individual creativity consistent with the Internet. But if it doesn't generate revenue for your company, it will be your butt on the line. And it will be your responsibility to let them down easy, explain to them that at the end of the day this is a business, not simply a spiritual experience. You will be unpopular. You will not be invited to share herbal tea with them at break time. That's the sort of real-world test that makes understanding this change important.

Keeping a happy workforce is especially important if you are an IT manager. The competition for technology people remains the battleground in the dot-com world. Recruiting, training, and retaining these folks is an expensive proposition, so you have to be accommodating. You also have to beg and grovel and bribe. For example, a friend of mine negotiated an all-expenses-paid Caribbean vacation trip for himself and his family simply for agreeing to go for a first interview at a Silicon Valley dot-com. And to think that when I was looking for a job, I was happy if the HR people called me back.

Corporate Toadies beware. Learn from my experience at the consulting seminar. The world has changed, for better or worse, but it has changed. The arrogance of the boomer generation is passé. It is a liability. It is a tailbone, an appendix. It serves no purpose any more, but it can cause pain when bruised or inflamed. Indeed, it can cause embarrassment. Big titles are vestiges of those times when dinosaurs roamed the earth. That would be the 1980s, when we were all too busy consuming conspicuously and congratulating ourselves on the fact that we had more earning power than any other group in history to notice what was really going on.

Now, you may have trouble with all of this coddling. Not that it's impossible to adjust, but if you are set in your ways about what work is and how an employee should relate to a company, you have to get rid of that thinking. Loyalty is admirable, but it is old economy. And it is out of step with the dot-com environment. And the traditional trappings of corporate loyalty have lost all currency.

Still, you Dot-Com Dynamos shouldn't be too quick to claim victory. Because you've got some adjusting to do, too. The gold rush of the early days is over. The future phases of the dot-com economy are all about hard work and accountability. There is less opportunity to job-hop because there are fewer places to which to hop. There are not a lot of discretionary development budgets around that will allow you to throw stuff against the wall and see if it sticks. Sure, you will still be able to pick and choose the companies to which to lease your services, especially if you are at all technically adept. But the balance of power has shifted somewhat. You will have to be regulated a little more than perhaps you would like. In short, the zookeepers are back in charge.

The same goes for the Desperately Seeking Somethings. Recalibrate those expectations. Reality is now part of the virtual world.

The people in the best position here are you Closet Creatives. You have a strong sense of loyalty, mainly because it means security. But you are open and flexible, too. Your view of loyalty will become the model for the next phase of the dot-com world. It will be balanced. Not too much of one thing or the other. Just right. So pick up the ball. Make up your own title.

chapter four

On Bosses

I had a boss once at the *New York Times* who didn't look at people when he talked to them. And I don't mean he was a little shy and diverted his eyes up or down or sideways during a conversation. I mean, it was as if this guy's head was on sideways. I spent my job interview talking to his left ear. For an hour. He would direct questions to his desk lamp, and the sounds would bounce off the bookcase and the far wall, and come back to me. I would respond, at length and in great detail, to the side of his head. It was sort of like sitting in the backseat of a taxicab, trying to figure out whether you should talk to the driver's reflection in the rearview mirror or to the back of his neck. Afterward, exhausted from the experience, I asked colleagues whether he was deaf. No, I was told, he was just odd. But a great journalist, nonetheless. I had learned over the years that the two often went hand in hand.

I had another boss who tried to throw off people by playing the crazy-professor/third-world-dictator role. He would roam the office halls in his sock feet, puffing on two cigarettes at once, stroking his ponytail, and yelling about our incompetence. "If this were a nuclear reactor," he would bellow, "we'd all be blown to hell by now." He would fit right in at a dot-com.

I had another boss who would tug at his underwear during times of stress. On particularly bad days, he would yank and pull at his briefs so vigorously that he would often rip them. At the very least, they would become so tight around his vitals that he would address people in a soprano pitch. High voice, high anxiety. It was a signal to all of us to keep our heads down.

Or there was the sneaky boss who would leave me reprimands on voice mail in the middle of the night, then make herself unavailable to meet for days after so I couldn't respond in person. I think she's in prison now. Or the Hamptons. Somewhere where those types of people end up.

Anyway, everyone has a nightmare boss story. It's part of work life. Ever since the days of Ebenezer Scrooge, the Bob Cratchetts of the world have lived cursed lives at the hands of their bosses. Doing their bidding. Kissing their butts. And all for a pittance of a salary and the odd pat on the head.

And it's no different in the dot-com world. In fact it may be worse, for many reasons. There is a dearth of great management talent, and there are changing views of authority, hierarchy, and loyalty. There is even a new view workers have of their own responsibilities to their employers and to themselves. And the whole space is so new that everyone is feeling their way.

In the early days, too, there was not much need for great management. Or at least that was the perception. As long as Wall Street was throwing money at dot-com companies, and shoppers were logging on, and stock prices continued to rise, why bother? Why screw with a good thing? Laissez faire. Que sera, sera. Rock on. In those heady days of do-no-wrong, a monkey could have run a dot-com company. Indeed, many did just that.

— ◆ —

It was a signal to

all of us to

keep our heads down.

— ◆ —

I met several in my travels. One, in particular, was the perfect example of the "Party on, dude" style of management that had set the dot-com world apart from the old economy. He spent every waking hour trying to get on television or being on television. And he made his staff spend all of their time getting him on television.

It was remarkable, really, this singular focus of his. Getting him to talk to employees or investment analysts or print journalists or any other constituent who was important to the company was like pulling teeth. He would always find some scheduling conflict that would prohibit him from participating in these other sessions.

But if CNBC or CNN called asking for his opinion on any-thing—whether it was related to the company or the industry or not—he would clear his calendar and race to the nearest studio. Even when a producer called to fact-check a story, this guy would ask if there was any need for him to go on camera to clarify the point. Often, he wouldn't even wait to be asked. He would call for a car and have it take him directly to the studio, where he would barge into the newsroom and pitch himself to the reporters and the producers.

I remember asking him once if he wasn't overexposing himself a little. Like the boy who cried wolf, he tried to make news so many times when there wasn't any that when he actually had something important to say, no one listened. The concept was lost on this talking airhead.

"It's all about impressions," he told me. "That's all people remember. They don't care what you say, because they won't remember it. But they will remember your face."

I guess I don't need to tell you that he was a marketing guy, consumed (as many are) by his own star quality—or more precisely, the star quality he believed he possessed. He had no idea what he was talking about, on or off the air. He had no idea about the difference between paid media and editorial media, and the relative credibility viewers place on each. To him, they were the same, with the same power, the same oomph, the same capacity to vault him into the stratosphere of Internet guru-dom. People who saw him on television didn't remember what he said because he spoke nonsense. And they remembered his face only because it was ubiquitous. At one point his close advisers thought that he was spending so much time on

CNBC that they would offer him a job as an anchor. At least that's what everyone hoped would happen.

Indeed, everyone was disappointed (but not surprised) instead when he made a movie starring himself. Using company money and company resources. He called it a defining moment for the company. Sort of an online *Spartacus*. The working title among his closest associates was "Blowhard."

— ◆ —

In the early days of dot-com, you could afford to act up a little more.

— ◆ —

Alas, his kind was not the exception but the rule in the early days of the Internet. Every man, woman, or child (and I am not exaggerating here) who could sit upright in an office chair and look into a television camera for three or four minutes was a media darling. At meetings or lunches or cocktail parties, executives who showed up without the pancake makeup used in television studios to cut down facial glare were shunned. If you couldn't drop the first names of the anchors on CNBC—like Ron or Sue—you were out of the loop. If you weren't talking to Lou—as in Lou Dobbs, former anchor on the old CNN Moneyline—earlier in the day, you were bush-league. Words like "loser" would be muttered up and down through the ranks to describe you.

But all that posturing was fine, because back in those early days of the Internet, it didn't matter. As I said, you could put a monkey on the air and your company's stock would go up. Many companies did just that.

In the early days of the Internet, the quality of management wasn't so much of an issue internally, either. From an employee's point of view, if you didn't like your boss, you could leave, because there were always lots of other opportunities inside and outside your company. You could get away with leaving because you thought your boss was a jerk. In many cases, though, it wasn't that bosses were jerks; it was just that they weren't very good bosses. They had no training, no experience. They were thrust into positions of authority and told to do their best. Many didn't even know what their best was.

I remember getting a call from a young friend who after only three months at an Internet company was promoted to vice president. Fifty people reported to him, some of them older than he was. He had a budget of several million dollars. He had agencies, vendors, and affiliates to manage. He reported directly to the CEO and was placed on the executive committee of the company, a policy-making, rules-and-regulations-shaping body made up of the senior-most decision makers. He didn't know whether to laugh or cry. He was twenty-six.

"What do I do now? What do I do first?" he asked me, quaking in his boots. "I always thought I'd get here, just not this fast."

I didn't have much real-world advice for him. I was more than ten years older than he was, and I had only a fraction of his responsibility in my old-economy job. I hadn't been where he was. I told him to read Tom Peters and Peter Drucker. Right away. Oh, and to pray.

In those early days, you could also afford to act up a little more than you might in a tough job market, be outraged, and storm out, no matter how big or small the issue. You could always find another job. Or, you could always come back to the job you left, because the company probably would have grown enough to accommodate your return. And the person you yelled at was probably not there any more—either gone to another dot-com or promoted even higher.

These days, as the Internet is going through a transition, it's time for everyone to cool that temper. Don't be so impetuous. You may have to put up with the kooks and the psychos in charge, but consider the alternative: unemployment. Learning to exist and excel under bad bosses is one of the most valuable skills you can acquire. And believe me, bad bosses are not exclusive to any economy, any industry, or any kind of company. They are everywhere, and dot-coms are no exception.

This is where you Corporate Toadies and Closet Creatives have an advantage. Chances are you have had experience with crazy bosses, driven by power and trapped by hierarchy, a dangerous, combustible combination. You have seen what ambition and pressure can do to them, and to the people they manage. You have seen the ruthlessness that comes with even a smidgen of authority in the wrong hands. You have seen how power corrupts even the most unlikely suspects. You may have been one of these people yourself.

If you're in a dot-com already, you may have already felt the sea change in management. The stars and starlets of the

Internet's marketing age have faded with the dawn of the new day of accountability. The party's over. The new faces in the executive suites are real, legitimate management types, many of them brought in from old-economy companies to sort through the rubble and rebuild. Watch your step with these people. They are not indulgent. And they are under enormous pressure from a lot of different places to turn things around, quickly. They will not put up with any of your guff.

If you're Desperately Seeking Something, and just coming into the dot-com workforce, remember that you've got a good resource to help you understand what's happening on this front. People like me, who have lived through the wars. And if you do seek me out, I ask only this favor: Look at me when you're talking to me.

While we're on this topic, let's look at discipline. It is the big stick with which bosses exercise, protect, and expand their authority. Because in the dot-com world, where authority and hierarchy and loyalty are in flux, discipline takes on a whole new dimension.

I had a boss in the old economy who would discipline me in a most peculiar way: She would hand me a memo or a report or a letter I had written and make me change the tenses. If it was written in past tense, my task was to change it to the present. Or vice versa. If it was conditional, it would become declarative. If it was written in passive voice, then active voice it must be.

Do you remember *Cool Hand Luke*? Where Paul Newman had to dig a hole, then fill it in. Then dig the hole again, and fill it in, over and over. While the fat warden and the guard with the aviator shades looked on. Well, I was in an office job version of that scene. I was "shakin' it up here, boss," only it was with a ballpoint pen, not a shovel.

Of course, it was an exercise in pointlessness. The final copy of the document would go out in its original form. Just the way I had drafted it in the first place. I knew it. She knew it. But she was the boss and, well, she was the boss. There was really no wiggle room at all.

— ◆ —

If you do something wrong, your "thought partner" can turn into the Marquis de Sade in a heartbeat.

— ◆ —

It drove me nuts. And I vowed that after she died, I would one night sneak into the graveyard where she was buried and edit her tombstone.

Still, I have to give her credit. It was a smart if treacherous method of making me pay for whatever I had done to displease her. Smart, because she picked something that I loved to do—write—and rubbed my nose in it. Sort of like asking Michelangelo to repaint the Sistine Chapel with a spray can. Oh, all right. Maybe more like making the guy who drives the Zamboni machine at Madison Square Garden drive clockwise instead of counterclockwise when resurfacing the ice.

The point is that discipline takes many shapes and forms, depending on the boss and the nature of the indiscretion. And in the old economy, it was easy to administer. Because the old economy, with its hierarchy and respect for authority, lent itself perfectly to a culture of discipline. Boss—underling. Warden—inmate. Master—slave. One held the authority; the other submitted to it. Disobedience meant punishment. And punishment set an example for other subordinates. It was an effective method of control, but only if everyone understood and agreed to his or her role in the scheme.

Now, unless you have the will of a Cool Hand Luke, you probably respond well to discipline if you are a true Corporate Toady. You accept the fact that you are the subordinate, and if you do something wrong, you are repentant. It is more a matter of survival than anything else. I mean, what's the point of living at odds with your boss, no matter how awful he is? He's the boss. Say you're sorry, do your time, and promise that whatever you did won't happen again. Believe me, that's all they want to hear. I'm a boss now, too, and that's all I want to hear. That it won't happen again. That I won't be bothered with the same stupid problem one more time.

If you're the litigious type, you always have the OSHA option. When I was in the newspaper business, our people kept OSHA busy with endless complaints about carpal tunnel syndrome, the painful debilitating condition that results from the repetitive strain on muscles and joints from using a computer keyboard for extended periods of time. There were lawsuits, and there were threats of lawsuits. Of course, for every legitimate case of the disorder, there were a dozen sympathetic cases. Everyone knew it.

Let's just say this. An OSHA complaint is a great way to blow off some steam and get some time off. But let me give you a little hint: No matter what they tell you about an OSHA complaint having no adverse effect on your opportunities for advancement, they are lying. You can forget about that promotion, that raise. You can probably forget about an invitation to the Christmas party, too. You are radioactive. You aren't going anywhere.

And for God's sake, don't cry. Please, don't. There is nothing that will bring more wrath upon you than crying about being disciplined. I wish I had a bullet for every person, man or woman, who cried in my office about everything from a lost hamster to an annual meeting gone awry. Get a grip. It's a job, not cancer. Save the tears for something that matters.

But discipline is not so easy in the dot-com world, because of the absence of strict hierarchies and the blurred lines of authority. And because of terms like "thought partner." I'm not making this up. The expression "thought partner" really does exist. It is a wonderfully inclusive term that gives employees the impression that they actually share common goals with their bosses, and that together, the whole is greater than its parts. It's sort of a corporate mind-meld. And it is used by recruiters endlessly, trying to convince prospects that they aren't being asked to come to work at the company so much as they are being asked to join a Lennon-McCartney-esque collaborative effort.

And if you believe this, it is clear that you are in your first job. The idea of a thought partner is the product of an idealism so absurd, even in the dot-com world, that it defies comprehension. Don't be stupid. Don't be naive. Of course you have a boss. And that boss decides whether you live or die professionally. If something screws up, if you do something wrong, your thought partner will turn into the Marquis de Sade in a heartbeat. You can't change human nature, even in an organic world like the Internet. It's every person for himself—or herself. It's the law of nature.

O.K., maybe you should start crying, after all.

chapter five

On Accountability

S omeone should teach a physics course in business school. You know, physics. For every action there is an equal and opposite reaction. You drop a penny into a glass full of water and the water overflows. You place a weight on one end of a beam balanced at its fulcrum and the other end is elevated.

It's the same in life. For every action there is a reaction. You pull your little sister's hair; she cries and tells mom. You ask a woman who is much better looking than you out on a date and she says no. You ask your husband to get his butt off the sofa and take out the trash and he snores louder. These are basic laws of nature.

And this cause-and-effect principle applies to business, too, at least to old-economy business. In the traditional company, you design a good product and sales go up. You design a crappy product and sales go down. The CEO discovers that you are responsible for the design of the crappy product and you are fired. There are consequences to the action and the reaction. There is responsibility. Accountability.

Well, the law of physics doesn't apply in the dot-com world. You spend a lot of money to design a great product and not only do sales not go up, you become a guru, too. You spend a lot of money to design a crappy product, and chances are, no one says boo! And if someone does say boo! you say, so what? There's more where that came from.

— ◆ —

Is it acceptable to use

skateboards and bicycles

in the office?

— ◆ —

I wrote a speech not long ago for the chief financial officer of a dot-com company on the challenges faced by an e-CFO—that's shorthand for an e-commerce CFO. The speech was to be delivered to an audience of more than 500 people, most of them dot-com finance executives who were struggling with the odd dynamics of e-commerce that affected the age-old discipline of bean counting.

It was a pretty fun assignment, because the topic allowed a little more freedom than the usual finance-related stuff. We weren't focused on things like the balance sheet or market capitalization. We looked at some of the weird things that a CFO has to be prepared for when stepping into the dot-com space.

Some of the challenges were pretty obvious. The huge expenditures needed for technology, and the difficulty nontechnical people like CFOs have understanding what's really important. As the CFO said, sometimes technology people tell you that their projects are more complicated than they really are, because the more complicated they are, the more they will cost. And you really have no way of knowing whether they're scamming you or not. You simply assume they are.

We also looked at peculiarities of the dot-com workplace. Like trying to figure out how to budget for on-site basketball courts or yoga rooms, or any number of other perks that are the building blocks of the dot-com world. Like whether the building in which you have offices allows dog care. That's no typo. It's dog care, as in day care, but for pooches. And whether it was acceptable for skateboards and bicycles to be used in the office, to go from meeting to meeting, and if so, how much needed to be spent on storage racks.

We also explored how the Internet had rewritten the accounting rules, because the business models were so different from earlier ones that it was difficult to value companies. Therefore, new measures and new metrics were created, some of them legitimate, some of them not. It was a challenge for everyone to determine which was which.

But the biggest challenge we identified was accountability. Of all the bugaboos in the Internet space, this was the buggiest. Mainly because accountability didn't exist.

Not in the traditional sense, anyway. Consequences, responsibility? Those were terms from the old economy. In a world where ideas and funding is limitless, accountability be damned. Spend the money. Throw it up against the wall and see if it sticks. If it does, great. If it doesn't, who cares? Try something else.

For a finance person, this kind of attitude was a nightmare. If you wonder what keeps dot-com finance people up at night, it's this kind of thinking. Who's going to pay for all those great ideas, especially the ones that aren't going to generate revenue? It didn't seem to register with the dotcoms that if you robbed Peter often enough to pay Paul, someday Peter was going to be broke. Well, Peter's broke now, and Paul's somewhere in the Caribbean, laughing his butt off.

When it comes to accountability, the marketing people are even worse than the IT people. That's one of the few similarities between the old and the new economy. In the online world, the amount of money spent on advertising and marketing with little or no results to show is outrageous. This was especially true in the early days, when most Internet companies couldn't get a product delivered to a customer. Some still can't.

I mean, what were they thinking? Who was paying attention when the ad agency put together a national campaign for an e-commerce Web site that featured gerbils being shot from a cannon into a plywood target? Huh? And you want me to give these guys my credit card? You want me to share with them personal information about my preferences and my tastes? You want me to be in their database as a customer, and when someone searches gerbils, my name pops up alongside that guy from *An Officer and a Gentleman*?

No thanks.

Let's just say that the guys at Pets.com who came up with the sock puppet as spokesperson had the right idea. Not only did it capture the imagination of a whole bunch of people, it also saved the company principals from ever being recognized, and it now allows them to eat in public without being stoned by shareholders whose investments evaporated when the company went under.

Corporate Toadies know what I'm talking about. Accountability has been a requirement of your career since day one. If you do something that works, you expect to get credit. If you do something that doesn't work, you expect to accept blame. Lucky you. This will be one of the most important credentials in the dot-com world. It will carry you to great success if you make it priority number one. It's the kind of word that will get you in good with the new senior management group that is moving into dot-com. Don't simply give them ideas. Give them ideas that will pay for themselves, with a little something left over that they can call profits.

Closet Creatives beware. Don't compromise on this one, even though compromising is one of the things you do best. Don't try to pass the buck, or obfuscate the truth.

Desperately Seeking Somethings beware, too. Resist the temptation to shirk accountability and blame someone else. It is one of your great strengths to redirect blame. Three years ago, you could have easily gotten away with that in the dot-com space. Now, you wouldn't last a minute.

But the biggest lesson is to be learned by the Dot-Com Dynamo. You must pay attention to this. Chances are that until now you have mastered the weasel approach to account-ability. You have stepped up brazenly to take credit for victories, but quickly disassociated yourself from things that didn't work. Yet you have let others know that you are observant and aware of failures. You may have cast suspicion elsewhere without pointing fingers. You stole your rallying cry from Bart Simpson: "It was broken when I got here." A couple of years ago, that attitude would have made you dot-com management material, no question about it. Today, it's "later, dude."

—◆—

If you can replace, "Good morning, Mr. Phelps," with a simple grunt, you save an entire nanosecond.

—◆—

Along with accountability come certain behavior patterns that will become increasingly important in the next generation of dot-com. They are marks of responsibility, maturity. Together, they spell management material.

Remember grammar school? (If you can't, you might consider a line of work other than a dot-com.) Do you recall how you were taught very early the basics of polite social behavior? Look people in the eye when you speak to them. Speak clearly and concisely so people can hear you. Respect your elders. Address them by Mr., Mrs., or Miss.

Say please, thank you, and excuse me at the appropriate times. With peers, the directive was "play nicely; share your toys."

Then there were the basics of hygiene and organization. Keep yourself and your room neat and tidy. Pick up after yourself. That sort of thing.

If you're a guy, you were probably also taught all the stuff that got thrown out with the advent of feminism and sexual harassment lawsuits. Like opening doors and holding chairs for women. Lighting their cigarettes, back when smoking wasn't a felony. Complimenting women on their appearance.

Yes, there was certain gentility to the age of manners. But it's all ancient history now. In the dot-com world, everything is casual, from the dress to the hours, to the look of the workplace, to the way people interact with each other. Not that it's all bad, mind you. There are some conventions that needed to die. Like dance cards.

But did we have to throw it all out? Or did it just slip away while we weren't looking? Or more likely, was formality considered an impediment to efficiency? In other words, if I can dispense with the salutation, "Good morning, Mr. Phelps," and replace it with "Hi," or even better, a simple grunt that does not require the forming of even a contracted word, I have saved an entire nanosecond. And if, in every encounter I have every day, I employ this clever trick, I can save a whole second, maybe more. Over a year, that's, well, a lot of seconds. Over a career, it's an eternity.

If you're not a Dot-Com Dynamo, get used to it. In dot-com, you have entered the Land of Grunts. Now those of you who are parents are probably saying that the dot-com world does not corner the market on grunts. Talk to any teenagers and you will see there is a whole rich deposit of grunts, untapped and waiting to be mined.

Of course, that's where it starts. Amazing that in a culture where we surround ourselves with media that presumably should encourage communication, we are ourselves losing the ability to communicate. Now I'm not going to go into the sociological reasons behind the decline and fall of the verbal skills of our youth, and who is responsible. But I will say this. We could all use a little formality, now and again.

And so could dot-com. I was in a dot-com CEO's office when another senior manager stopped by with a job candidate. The kid was good, the manager raved. Top of his class. Could make computers do stuff you wouldn't believe.

The CEO rose from his chair when they entered and extended his hand. "Great to meet you," he said.

"Hey" was the only response from the kid. And his hands remained deep in his pants pockets. He didn't look nervous or shy or overwhelmed by the situation. He simply looked clueless.

It was an awkward moment for everyone. The CEO took his outstretched hand and smoothly put it on the kid's shoulder, an Eleanor Roosevelt move if ever there was one. The manager who was offering up the kid as a prospect tried to smooth the waters. "Josh here is tired. Came in on the red-eye from California. Probably has trouble keeping his eyes open right now."

Uh-huh. To me, it looked like Josh had just consumed his body weight in metamphetamines. But then the conversation quickly turned to macroservers and excess processing capacity and I was left in the dust.

So what, you say? Not important. Who cares whether Josh doesn't know or care about the importance of a handshake, which is an old-economy ritual anyway? If the kid can light up that Web site, social polish is irrelevant.

Well, right or wrong, it rubs me the wrong way. The same way that people who butt into lines at the movies, or at the grocery store, or the dry cleaner rub me the wrong way. And it will rub you the wrong way if you're a traditional manager who is used to a minimum standard of social behavior. There's a reason this stuff is called "common" courtesy. It is usual, or it should be. It isn't "special" or "extraordinary" courtesy, only to be rolled out at Grandma's house, or, perhaps the CEO's office.

Now I'm not suggesting that formality necessarily has to mean stiff and stuffy. But I am suggesting that there is something very wrong with the Land of the Grunts. Call me stuck up. I don't care. I think people like a little ceremony. And here's a secret. I think dot-comers welcome it.

I tried an old trick in the new economy recently, with surprising results. When I was a journalist, one of my bosses had a habit of dropping people handwritten notes, either complimenting them on work or suggesting ways to do something better. As the world became more electronic, these little notes became refreshing treasures. Different. Useful. Special. Reporters who had just finished big stories eagerly awaited the little thick bonded envelopes, with the monogrammed notepaper inside, and the words of encouragement scrawled in the unmistakable bright blue ink of a fountain pen.

There are still a few senior executives who use this method. Jack Welch, the chairman of General Electric, is one. Don Marron, the chairman of PaineWebber, is another. Al Siegel, a senior editor at the *New York Times,* writes his in green ink. They're known at the *Times* as "greenies," and while they're often as critical as they are complimentary, they are far better read than any interoffice memo.

I tried it one day, to see if I would get any reaction at all. I dropped a colleague a note, handwritten, complimenting him on raising an important issue in a meeting and suggesting that he had saved the company a good deal of embarrassment. Not long after I sent the note, he was at my door.

"What a great idea," he said, waving the notepaper. "Do you do this all the time?"

No, but I will from now on. Of course, I could have sent exactly the same message by e-mail to his desktop PC or laptop or text pager. And it would have arrived in a fraction of the time. But it would have been just another line of blue type in his directory, along with hundreds of such messages that accumulate in his e-mailbox every day.

Funny how an old, formal method can cut through the clutter of the electronic age. But that's the point, and it's an important one if you want to be effective in the dot-com world. As the technology has become pervasive, people have become lazy. Not so much in body as in mind. It's too easy to let the machines do the work, do the thinking. It's too easy for people to become processors of information, not communicators of ideas.

If you're an old-economy manager, you can make hay on this. Instead of writing an e-mail to a colleague, get out from behind your computer and plunk yourself down in his office. Talk to him, face-to-face. And when you leave, shake his hand, thank him for his time. He may think it's a great new way to communicate. And if it's new, you can bet everyone will try it.

Along with accountability comes the harsh reality that you can't always get what you want. That all the funky stuff that dot-coms have become famous for are no longer

—◆—

Such intangibles are difficult to explain to shareholders who are wondering when the bottom line will change color.

—◆—

givens. If you are managing a dot-com, you know that there is no secret to this. It has to do with costs. Perks cost money. And while their benefits may be real, such intangibles are difficult to explain to shareholders who are watching the bottom line, wondering when it will change color.

The balance between creating an attractive workplace and doing so on a shoestring is one of the most painful side effects of accountability. If you are seeking a job in dot-com, or are managing there already, here is a cautionary tale.

I interviewed a candidate not long ago for a position at a dot-com company. The woman was bright, poised, professional. Her credentials were impeccable: advanced degree from a good school, a few years' experience under her belt, good references. She was well-spoken, amiable, and had a good sense of humor—all qualities that would make her an ideal hire, and a potential manager. I was encouraged that someone like this would consider working in dot-com.

We talked for a while about her background and picked apart the job description for the open position. We talked broadly about the structure of the company, the culture, the career opportunities. We examined the compensation package. All the usual interview stuff. Then, the talk turned to benefits. We had a great plan, I explained. Medical, dental, vision care, long-term disability, life insurance, and so on and so on.

She stopped writing and put down her pen. "That's it?" she asked, looking disappointed.

"Of course not," I replied, "you get all major holidays off, generous vacation, and personal day allowances. If you're sick, no problem, we're pretty flexible. And if a family member dies, you get three days' grief allowance."

Sounded pretty fair to me. But she still looked unhappy. "And perks? What about perks?"

I laughed. "Well, we have fresh coffee in the cafeteria every morning, free of charge, and once in a while Margie over in accounting bakes cookies. We all like the peanut butter chip best." I thought that was a good answer.

She didn't. "No, I'm talking about perks. You know, like massages. Oh yes, and another thing: Can I bring my dog to work?"

I had to admit to this candidate that although we offered some added niceties, like baskets of fresh fruit and yoga classes, we did not have a wide array of these other perks. The environment had changed. What was true even six months earlier was no longer so. Even the trappings of the Internet world were disappearing in Internet time. She was disappointed, to be sure. She said she would think about the job.

If you're a traditional manager, get ready for this one. It is a big issue. Workplace environment. And I don't simply mean a workplace free of bias based on race, religion, age, sex, nationality. I don't mean a place where everyone has an equal opportunity to advance, where employees can work without fear for their safety or their sanity. And I certainly don't mean a workplace where free coffee and the odd magazine subscription are considered perks.

No, I'm talking about a workplace that is fun, fulfilling, challenging. Cool, hip, happening. A workplace about which employees can boast to their friends. An office environment that is a status symbol in itself that says, basically, *I rule.*

And to do it all in an environment of smaller budgets and increased demands for efficiency.

Now before you say, "No way, I'm not going to buy into this sort of indulgence," let me say this: You have no choice on this one. Trust me.

Remember what we learned about the relationship that members of the dot-com generation have with their employers? They are doing us a favor by showing up for work. We should be thankful that we are allowed to pay them a salary and give them stock options, in return for sharing their skills with us. They could take those skills anywhere, share them with anyone. It's sad, but true.

What will make them choose your company is the other stuff. The perks. If your dot-com doesn't even have a couple of modest ones, get them. Forget the cost if you can. Take it out of the marketing budget. Better yet, take it out of the recruiting and training budget. Because these things are essentially recruiting tools. They are noncash bonuses. And remember, we live in a world where our role models are professional athletes and entertainers. They get all sorts of noncash compensation that makes their work lives more comfortable, more productive.

The point is that a work environment that offers opportunities for advancement and for learning is *assumed* in the dot-com world. They aren't special draws; they're givens. So you need a little extra.

Frankly, if you're the entrepreneurial type looking for a new opportunity, I think it lies right here, in the growing market for unique perks that don't cost too much. That's it! DiscountPerks.com. Now where did I put the number for that venture capitalist?

chapter six

On the
Generation Gap

T hey say that in love and in hitting an inside curve-ball, timing is everything. The same goes for dot-coms. Though I have to say that given the choice, I would opt for the inside curve. Not that it's that much easier to deal with, but at least its path is somewhat more pre-dictable than those of the other options.

O.K., if you were paying attention, you would have noticed that I have fallen into a typical trap of traditionally trained managers: the sports metaphor. It's the kind of stuff that gets old-economy managers in trouble these days. It used to be that it only drove certain women nuts when they came into the workforce. Not-so-subtle sexism was the claim. Vestiges of the old boys' network. Exclusionary. Bad form. Bad boy.

Now, it's not just the women who don't understand. If you don't believe me, just go into the men's room of almost any dot-com company. Where are the copies of *Sports Illustrated*? *Golf Digest*? *Sporting News*? I'll tell you where they are: gone. Replaced like yesterday's news by stuff like *Wired, Internet Week,* and *Industry Standard.* HTML has replaced RBI in the daily lexicon around the cappuccino machine. Red Zone is a server capacity problem, not the prime real estate inside the twenty-yard line. Red Dog is a fancy beer, not a linebacker blitz.

— ◆ —

Do you feel like you were born too soon for the dot-com world?

— ◆ —

Anyway, if I lapse into sports-speak again, I apologize. I still haven't completely weaned myself of the practice. I mean, I am only human. I put on one skate at a time, like everyone else. I can't hit it out of the park every time. Can't throw the long bomb every play. Can't sink the fifty-foot putt every . . . Well, you get the idea.

But back to the issue of timing. If you were born too soon—if you are a Corporate Toady or even a Closet Creative—you may feel like you have missed a great opportunity in the dot-com world. Born too late—just now getting into the workforce? Same issue.

Indeed, a lot is made of age in the Internet. Too much, really, in my experience. But what do you expect, when the average age of dot-com employees is somewhere in the midtwenties, and the average age of management is an entire generation older? I might add that by traditional standards, a senior management group that averages in the midforties is considered extremely young. In the dot-com world, it is considered ancient.

When you take these two generations and jam them together in a new environment where there are no preconceived notions of what's right and what's wrong, there's bound to be confusion. Consider this: Most Internet companies are only a few years old. There is no culture, no precedent, no homegrown talent. Everything is new. Everyone is new.

Frankly, the fact that these two generations collided together and made the Internet grow is a feat in itself. It shows that given a common cause—in this case, the promise of untold riches overnight—anything is possible.

A dot-com colleague who had just turned twenty-five asked me about the three things I remembered vividly by the time I was her age. The answers were easy: the assassination of John F. Kennedy, man landing on the moon, and seeing Bob Gibson pitch for the St. Louis Cardinals in the 1968 World Series against the Detroit Tigers. (Not much happened in the '70s that was of interest to me, except maybe mood rings and the discovery of Jolt cola—twice the caffeine, twice the sugar.) But her choices reminded me of the gap: the Challenger space shuttle explosion, *Dirty Dancing*, and the death of Princess Diana.

The point of the exchange isn't that our lists were different. It's that the exchange happened at all. If ever there was an environment where people need not stand on ceremony, it is the dot-com world. The open concept of the dot-com in every sense—from lack of hierarchy to lack of walls and doors—means that people of any age can prosper.

The Internet is all about curiosity. Discovering new things about new things. If you're a traditional manager, it's all about discovering a twenty-something colleague who knows a hell of a lot more than you do about the latest technology. If you're that twenty-something geek, you may discover that the experience of that wrinkled old windbag down the way might just help you solve a problem you've been wrestling with for a while.

Now before I become the dot-com Dear Abby, let me just say this. The biggest hurdle for everyone in the dot-com world when it comes to age is getting over that preconceived notion of a generation gap. If you want, it need exist only in terms of the numbers printed on birth certificates or drivers' licenses. In dot-com, like in almost everything else, it's really your choice.

If you are somewhere in the middle of the age range, this is probably a little easier to understand. But those of you who are really old or really green, don't be afraid. Step up to the plate. Keep your eye on the ball. Keep that left elbow straight.

Oops. There I go again. Sorry.

By the way, you should know that I have never liked crystal balls. As a kid, I refused to play Ouija board with my brothers and sisters. It wasn't that I didn't have a healthy curiosity about what might happen in the future; it's that I didn't trust my sources.

Figuring out where your career is going to go is pretty much the same, as far as I'm concerned. It's a little bit luck, a little bit hard work, with a little bit of hocus pocus thrown in. You can set goals and expectations and impose some sort of measurement scheme to monitor your progress. But so much depends on where you are and what time it is in your life. It's a big consideration if you're leaning toward a dot-com company, especially now that the prospect of becoming a millionaire in a week or two is pretty much shot.

— ◆ —

The Internet is all

about curiosity.

— ◆ —

The CEO of an Internet company in California once gave me his take: "A career in the Internet is like gambling. Never bet more than you're willing to lose. And always have an exit strategy." Pretty sage for someone all of twenty-eight years old.

But he was right. There are a lot of risks at dot-coms for people of all ages. Ask anyone who has invested time and effort in a dot-com and has only a bucketfull of worthless stock options to show for it. Of course, for such people, things could be worse. Their company could have collapsed and they could be out of a job. For those unfortunate souls, the only other thing they have to show for their trouble is a line on their resume that says they worked for something that is now dead. Very hard on the old self-esteem.

With apologies to the young turks, I believe that risks of the dot-com world are far greater for the traditional manager. If you now have all the trappings of a corporate life, you may want to think twice about recalibrating your career plans. You need to consider the job security you require to pay a mortgage if you have one, support a family if you have one, send kids to college if you have them.

A friend of mine left a big job at a bank to become a finance officer at a dot-com. When it went out of business, he had to scramble to pay for his four-bedroom house and the costs of raising three teenaged children. He was sweating bullets about the first child going to college. When I last saw him, he was doing engineering inspections on houses. (I won't tell you his name because he knows about as much about house construction as I do. And that wouldn't fill a, you know, one of those sort of round things with the flat bottoms and . . . Well, you know what I mean.)

But I'm talking about the perks that many traditional companies offer to their management ranks. Like expense accounts. Car and clothing allowances. Club fees. Business class travel. There aren't a lot of dot-com companies around that can offer those kinds of perks to anyone other than the seniormost management. For a lot of traditional managers, especially in the more senior ranks, these are little comforts that may be hard to give up.

I can hear all you twenty-somethings playing the violins now. Very sad, you are saying. How can anyone live without a clothing allowance and a club membership? It's not that they can't; it's that those are things they may have strived for years to achieve. To them, these are the measurements of success, as absurd as they may seem to others just starting out in their careers. To each his own.

There is a bright side, though, for old-economy managers. The evolution of the Internet and the creation of so many new disciplines have whittled away at the concept of unemployability, especially when it comes to age. If you're in your forties or fifties or even sixties, and for whatever reason you have the desire to learn new skills that are relevant to the dot-com world, particularly in the IT area, come on in. The water's fine.

If you do decide to make the jump to dot-com, all I can say is be careful what you wish for. There is a screaming need for senior managers in the dot-com world right now. And not just marketing people who look good on television or can talk intelligently to a PowerPoint slide presentation. I mean people who have solid experience in managing companies, growing companies, and making them profitable. People who are not afraid to make the tough calls to cut costs and boost sales. People who in some measure must embody the kind of ruthlessness that has been absent in the dot-com world for so long.

The Catch-22: The reason there are a lot of opportunities is that it's an awful mess out there in dot-comland. A lot of the companies that didn't die in the latest wave of consolidation are still on life support. There is no guarantee that they will make it through the next crisis. Don't be surprised if the next want ad for a dot-com CEO includes this proviso: medical experience a plus.

If you're just starting out, the world is your oyster. Your career is ahead of you. You can afford to take a few risks. Be patient. The Internet is young. And like any youngster, it has to feel its way. It will bump into things, fall down, get cut and bruised. But it will keep getting up and moving forward. There will be great opportunities as the Internet grows and matures.

Still, in my experience, time has a funny way of playing tricks on you. And it can affect your view of the generation gap. One minute, you're plucking away on your bass guitar and singing killer lead vocals for "The Elliptic Horde" in the basement of your parents' house, and the next thing you know, you're telling your own kids to turn down that "Marilyn Manson crap" on the stereo. One minute, you're sneaking peaks at scenes from *Bob and Carol and Ted and Alice* on your parents' television, and the next you find X-rated movies sandwiched in between the Cartoon Network and Nick at Night—and no one seems to pay any attention.

Time is all about sensibilities. And no matter where you are in life, if you want to go to a dot-com, you're going to have to learn that time and sensibilities are different for everyone. This is not some sort of spiritual sermon. It is real advice on getting along in a dot-com work environment that is unlike any you've ever encountered before.

Here's what I mean. When the Beatles' album *Sgt. Pepper's Lonely Hearts Club Band* was released, I waited in line outside the record store overnight to get a copy. Me and a thousand other people. And this was in a small town. But the scene was played out in towns and cities across the country, and around the world.

Yessir, *Sgt. Pepper's* was big. No, really. As big as Windows 2000. John, Paul, George, and Ringo were huge. They were icons. Spokesmen for a generation.

So one day not long ago, I was working away in a dot-com office, listening to Napster, the online music service. And by the way, this sort of thing is O.K. in dot-comland. Listening to music while you work is sort of a nonevent. And if you can learn to concentrate on your work while you're listening, then you're on your way to multitasking. But we'll talk about that later.

— ◆ —

If you can learn to concentrate on your work while listening to music, you're on your way to multitasking.

— ◆ —

Anyway, I was listening to *Sgt. Pepper's* on Napster, and a young colleague popped into my office.

"Whatcha listening to?" he asked. "Oldies?"

Now to me, oldies means 1950s rock and roll. Chuck Berry. The Del Vikings. Anything from the *American Graffiti* movie soundtrack.

"No," I said, "It's the Beatles."

"Oh, yeah," my green friend replied. "I've seen John Lennon on those Fidelity Investment ads."

I took a deep breath. "Actually, it's Ringo and they're Charles Schwab ads. Remember, John Lennon died in 1980. He was shot to death just up the street . . ."

"Oh, yeah. Whatever."

Whatever. Whatever? Whatever!? John Lennon is not a "whatever." (O.K., Ringo Starr may be a whatever, but he was a Beatle. And he wins a couple of points for the Barbara Bach thing.) Still, I could have strangled this little weenie's neck. But I stopped.

Why? Because if the shoe had been on the other foot, and he had asked me to name Beck's latest CD, or to tell him the names of the band members in Blink 182 or 162 or whatever it is, I would have seemed just as disrespectful. And just as out of touch.

And if you think this kind of comparison only works in the rock and roll context, and is only applicable to old-economy managers and new-economy managers, consider Joe DiMaggio.

To my dad, he was Joltin' Joe, the Yankee Clipper, a star baseball player who to this day holds the major league record for getting hits in the most consecutive games. To my older sister, he was Marilyn Monroe's husband, so devoted that even after her death, he had flowers placed at her grave every day. To me, he was Mr. Coffee, a distinguished old dude with a white mane of hair who told the American television viewing public that they would get great-tasting coffee using the automatic drip machine that bore his stamp of approval.

To my "Beatle-challenged" dot-com colleague, Joe DiMaggio may just as well have been the director of *The Sopranos*.

No matter who you are, you must take all these factors into account when looking at life in a dot-com. Corporate

Toadies and Closet Creatives are probably most aware, because they know they are in foreign territory. They are aware that the big adjustments must come from them.

For the Desperately Seeking Somethings and the Dot-Com Dynamos, please be kind to the newcomers. Some stuff is important to people, no matter how dated it may seem to you. Remember, that Beatles fan was like you once. Cool, hip, on the cutting edge. And someday, someone will come along and ask you who the heck Kurt Cobain was.

And while we're here, let me, for the record, clarify something I said earlier that may be gnawing away at you. Joe DiMaggio is not the director of *The Sopranos*. Everyone knows it's Tommy LaSorda.

Of course, you can't bring up the name Joe DiMaggio without talking about heroes. It's simply un-American. Heroes provide interesting insight into the generation gap. Will Rogers said, "We can't all be heroes because someone has to sit on the curb and clap as they go by." They tell a lot about the people who choose them. About their aspirations, their inspirations. Mostly they give a little insight into where those doing the choosing fall short. I mean, isn't it true that you admire people who do stuff you can't do but wish you could? Go ahead, admit it. There's no one looking.

I'll admit it. My hero as a kid was Bob Gibson, a pitcher for the St. Louis Cardinals baseball club. I know. Pretty typical choice. Pretty pedestrian choice. But, hey, if you want to talk about your heroes, write me a letter.

Anyway, I liked Bob Gibson not only because he was a great baseball player, but because he was a great competitor. Now as a kid, I could throw a baseball pretty well. Good hard fastball. The natural curve that comes to a left-hander. The beginnings of a slider. But I didn't have Gibson's intensity, the kind of mastery, the intimidation, the total and complete control that he had on the mound. He didn't simply throw balls past the batters. He willed them into the catcher's mitt.

Man, I wanted to be able to stare down batters like he did, glaring out from under the bill of his cap, never wavering, never waffling. Overpowering, without showing off. All business, all the time.

In simple terms, he was good at his job. Or perhaps he was great at his job. And it's that quality that sticks with me now, years after he retired and I last picked up a baseball. Of course, I'll never have it. But I'll keep trying. Which is what it's all about.

So it's funny when you ask people who their heroes are, especially if the group being asked includes people from both sides of the dot-com generation gap.

When a number of traditional managers were asked to pick their heroes in business, many chose Jack Welch, chairman of General Electric. They liked him because he was tough, no-nonsense, not afraid to make difficult decisions, and a great deal maker. He thought structure was not only desirable, but necessary. Cuts of resources, including people, were essential sometimes for the good of the company.

If you're a Corporate Toady, you would probably be pretty comfortable with that choice. The chaos and lack of structure in the dot-com world would probably drive you nuts. And if you emulate Welch's style in the Internet space, someone may save you the trouble of blowing your brains out.

Fans of Bill Gates admired him for his creative as well as technical genius. He didn't simply create a new industry, he created a new culture at the same time. When these people spoke about Gates, it was equal parts admiration, emulation, and wonder.

— ◆ —

Everything you need to be an amazing success in the dot-com world Spiderman has.

— ◆ —

For Dot-Com Dynamos and the Desperately Seeking Somethings, you've probably got enough new economy juice in your veins to succeed. But resist the weird stuff that happens when some people talk about Gates. Remember, he's good, but he's not God. There's an extra "o" there that true disciples sometimes conveniently forget to include.

Which brings us to Spiderman again, which incidentally was the only real correct answer in the quiz I gave in the Introduction. Everything you need to be an amazing success in the dot-com world Spiderman has. He is fearless, he can climb buildings effortlessly, and he uses handheld devices effectively. He is old, yet he is youthful. He works well on his own, needs a minimum of direction, and understands the importance of accountability for his actions. And he's a funky dresser.

Most important, nothing fazes him. Come on, that's why he's a superhero. A madman planning to put cyanide in the city's water system? No problem. A runaway train loaded with plutonium heading for Grand Central Terminal? Piece of cake. A server exploding at a dot-com on the last week of shopping before Christmas, crashing the site and locking up customer service lines for hours? A walk in the park.

In fact, if you're looking for guidance on how to prepare for a dot-com job, here's a secret: Read a few Spiderman comics. No, really. It's better than any management book. It's better than a dozen hours cruising the message boards to find out what dot-coms are all about. You'll learn stuff that you can't even learn here. Like what superpowers are best suited for dot-com success. And the importance of a calm personality to balance all the excitement.

As for his funky outfit, I was only kidding. It is not appropriate for dot-com use. If only it came in black.

chapter seven

On Time and Space

I'm not really sure whether Einstein anticipated the dot-com world when he was conjuring up his theory of relativity, but it is clear that for the traditionally trained manager, the dot-com concepts of time and space are as difficult to decipher as $E = mc^2$.

Here's what I mean. When I moved from the old economy to the new, I took with me my daily routine. I arrived at the office about 7:30 A.M. and, if the day was relatively free of crises, I left around 6 P.M. For the first several weeks at the dot-com, I followed this routine. It was comfortable and familiar to me.

Until I realized that I was the only one in the building at 7:30 A.M., except for the mice. So I modified my schedule a little. I started arriving around eight. Still, I was alone. I tried 8:30, then 9 A.M. And still, I was talking only to myself. I started to worry. I couldn't really get to the office much later than that, because it would give me a pretty short workday if I left at six. And I was trained that a full and proper workday went from dawn to dusk.

But the idea of the day ending at dusk was a problem, too. I was at home one night about ten o'clock and the phone rang. It was someone from the office.

— ◆ —

Revolutionaries don't punch in on a time clock. They don't take rush hour trains to and from the revolution.

— ◆ —

"You know, we were just sitting around having lunch here at Starbucks, and we realized we hadn't run this idea past you," the fellow said. "Are you feeling O.K.? You went home so early."

I ignored the lunch comment, sensing it was added gratuitously for effect. But the time comment really burned me. "I get in at 7:30 A.M.," I snapped, "so going home at six isn't that early."

As soon as the words left my mouth I realized that I was missing the point. I was missing a fundamental difference between the old economy and the new. The sense of time in the dot-com world mirrors the medium that is its heart and soul: the Internet. It doesn't operate from nine to five. Nor do its people. Think about it. Revolutionaries don't punch in on a time clock. They don't move in traditional patterns. They don't take rush-hour trains to and from the revolution. The Insurgent Express? Absurd.

So whether you are a Corporate Toady, Closet Creative, or even a Desperately Seeking Something, you need some attitude adjustment. You need not only to view time differently, but to try to break habits that are defined by time. Like sleep. And eating. You also need some training in how time is used differently in the dot-com world, and how to use the tools needed to adapt to this new use.

Now we've all heard that an Internet year is really much shorter than an old-economy year. Some say it's three months long. Others say it's even shorter. Only part of the reason for this compression of time is the technology that allows the mass distribution of content with the push of a button. It's also about the changing concept of work time in the dot-com world.

Of course it helps that everyone is connected. Home offices, mobile communications like cell phones and pagers, and handheld devices like Palm Pilots make it easier to work 24–7 without feeling like you're tied to the office. Connectivity is efficient and freeing at the same time. If you believe that the best ideas are just as likely to happen at two o'clock in the morning on a deserted beach as at 10 A.M. in an oak-paneled boardroom, you get the point. And if you believe that the best ideas can *only* happen on that beach and at that time, you are probably a dot-com native. Hang onto that idea. It is a valuable one to carry with you no matter where you go in your career.

Of course, for the rest of us, adjusting to the mobile workplace is a challenge. First, we have to change our patterns. We have to listen more closely to our natural rhythms, which tell us our most creative times are not necessarily from nine to five. Some of us are more creative early in the morning, others late at night, and still others in the middle of the afternoon. (For those of you who are not creative at any time of the day or night, feel free to skip ahead to the chapter on fashion. It may stir some primal forces in you.)

I read this stuff somewhere about peak creativity varying by individual and tried to use it in my old job to explain why I was late with a financial report. "Terribly sorry, Mr. Big," I said confidently, "but my biorhythms were out of sync, and my creative peak did not coincide with the end of the fiscal quarter." Update for your career notebook: If you're in an old-economy company, use the "dog ate my homework" excuse instead of this one. It will save you a great deal of humiliation.

The point is, the sense of time in the old economy doesn't matter in the new economy. The expectation that we turn on a switch at nine o'clock and perform at peak through five o'clock is a fallacy. And it has nothing to do with whether you eat a big lunch, or drink a big lunch, or go to the gym at lunch. It's one of those unexplained mysteries of life that business has worked so hard to defy for so many years. Until, of course, the Internet came along and changed things.

All this is good news if you seek a dot-com position. The bad news is trying to figure out all the little devices we use to be connected, and thereby allowing our creative juices to flow anytime, anywhere. Right now, in my bag, I have a cell phone, a pager, a Palm VII, and a Blackberry. Aside from adding considerable weight collectively to my daily trek through the streets of New York City, they are a source of constant embarrassment and confusion.

Think VCR. Think a green 12:00 blinking, on and off, twenty-four hours a day. Must stop it. Can't stop it. Drives me crazy. Sometimes, I cover it with electrical tape, so I don't have to watch it. I'm convinced it was this cursed blinking green 12:00, not the black dog, that drove David Berkowitz to do what he did.

— ◆ —

On my commuter train every day, I watch the gray-suited old-economy types struggle through the mobile device ballet.

— ◆ —

Anyway, I can't program VCRs or electric coffeemakers or toaster ovens to begin with, so I am certain I use only a fraction of their capacity. The friendly and patient IT fellow at the office who answers my questions must wonder how long it took me to learn to use a conventional telephone. Worse, when one of my handheld devices chirps to life, I can never figure out which one is calling. I rip through my bag, checking each device in a frenzy. And nine times out of ten, by the time I find the right one, the caller/message is gone (I haven't figured out how to set up or retrieve messages, which probably comes as no surprise.)

Thankfully, I am not alone. On my commuter train every day, I watch the grey-suited old-economy types struggle through the mobile device ballet, fuming as they fumble with beeping, jingling, shrieking devices and wishing for the good old days when work-related calls came only one way: on the telephone. These guys are the ones who sit at home and cheer at that wine commercial on television, where all the yuppies throw their ringing cell phones into a pond, a symbolic gesture of the old economy that says connectivity is ruining my private life, not enhancing it.

Those people will never make it in the dot-com world. Because connectivity is all about making better use of time, and actually giving you more time, not taking it away. At least that's what they tell you. And I believe them. Unfortunately, learning how to save time through connectivity is actually consuming so much of my time right now that I have less time than I did before. But I will get better at it. I've invested a lot of money in these wretched things so I damn well better get better at it.

So, if you're like me, do yourself a favor. Learn how all these devices work. Seek help in setting them up properly, and use them to their capacity. Make them tools of creativity, not impediments. Use them to help you change the way you use time.

And if you're one of those people who knows how all these things works—a Dot-Com Dynamo and probably a lot of you Desperately Seeking Somethings—please take pity. Don't laugh too loud when you find out that the problem with a neophyte's Palm Pilot is that the batteries are dead. At least we're trying.

With a change in time comes a change in space—how it is used, when it is used, and why it is used. Both go through marked transformations in the dot-com world.

Let me give you an example. Try this: When I say nap room, what do I mean? No, this is not a typo. N-A-P, nap, as in snooze, sleep, rest. In the dot-com world, there are such things as nap rooms. And they are big deals. I learned about these products of the Internet while I was consulting for a dot-com company. I was in a meeting with a number of executives, and we were discussing budgets. The topic turned to workplace improvements. The question was put to the group: "And how much are we going to spend on that nap room?"

Had I heard correctly? Did someone just say nap room? I stuck my finger in my ear to see if there was wax or lint or paper in it. I looked around the table, hoping someone might see my confusion and help me out. No luck. They seemed serious about this.

I thought hard for a minute. A nap room. Hmmmm. Must be some sort of lounge where people who stay late at work can rest. Yes, that's it. It's a "stay-late-at-work" perk for those really busy times. Interesting idea. Very progressive.

The chief financial officer piped up: "Do we really need one? I mean, shouldn't these people nap on their own time? We could really put the money to better use."

Better use. The words crashed onto the table like a lead Zeppelin.

"This is an essential tool," said a young manager. "We need these places to be productive, to be creative. Rest is an important part of work."

I chuckled, then quickly turned it into a cough when I realized that no one thought that comment was the least bit absurd. "Rest is an important part of work?" Oh, please. Like Wales is an important part of Great Britain. Or vermouth is an important part of a very dry martini. Yet no one seemed to acknowledge the absurd contradiction. I must still have been missing something.

O.K., I thought, maybe nap rooms are places where work actually gets done. They must just be more casual than the meeting rooms I was used to. The word "nap" is just a way of poking fun at a culture that is different. Foolishly, I piped up.

Had I heard correctly?

Did someone just say nap room?

"What exactly is a nap room," I asked. "And what exactly is the purpose?"

Wow. I might as well have been speaking Klingon. The looks of disbelief consumed me. They said, who let this Neanderthal in the door? And are we actually paying him for his counsel?

Nap rooms, it was explained to me, were places where employees could snooze during the workday. They could take meetings in there, if they wanted, but that really wasn't the prime use. They could invite outsiders, like clients or vendors, in for naps, too, but only if it did not disturb other employees. But mostly, they were for employees to nap, sleep, catch a few winks, saw logs.

I imagined making this phone call: "Yea, Bob, listen I loved your proposal on the new back-end server enhancements, and I was wondering if you wanted to come over for a nap before we go over the budget."

O.K., narrow thinking, right? I mean, who's to say that napping doesn't improve productivity. And who's to say that doing a business deal in repose is any less effective than, say, doing it on the golf course or the tennis court. Maybe nap rooms are the secret weapons of the Internet.

By the way, if you know how to budget for a nap room, or a climbing wall, or any of the other "essential tools" of the dot-com workplace, you could be the chief financial officer of an Internet company, no problem. But would you want to be?

The point of all this is that patterns in the new economy are different than in the old economy. And for most people, patterns are very important. They provide security. Routine gives people reference points in their busy, chaotic lives. It gives them something to look forward to, even if it's something simple, like a cigarette after lunch or walking the dog before bed. I am not telling you anything new when I say that the human animal is a creature of habit.

Patterns afford sanctuary. They can invigorate, recharge. They can help clarify thoughts, solve problems. For example, I do my more creative thinking when I take a walk, or a little jog, not when I'm behind a desk. There's something about the physical activity that clears my head, gets my juices going. I really miss the experience if, for whatever reason, time does not allow it on a daily basis.

Places, too, have significance for patterns. Traditional managers like me have been taught that there are proper places to do things, or perhaps I should say appropriate places to do things. When you eat, you eat in a kitchen or

"You've got bad karma, dude. Chill."

a dining room (or more recently, any room that has a television). When you sleep, you sleep in a bedroom. When you bathe, you bathe in a bathroom. In the old days, you recreated in a rec room. When you have a business meeting, you meet in a meeting room. See how most all of these places are named for the activity that is performed inside them? Makes sense, doesn't it?

The dot-com workplace has introduced some variations on patterns and places. In the old days, the water cooler was the informal meeting place. Sort of the nap room of days gone by. If you wanted to bitch about something, you went for a coffee or a cigarette with a colleague. Now you hop online and air your beefs in an e-mail, a chat room, or on a message board. You want to go off-site to cut a deal or schmooze with a contact? Chances are it will be at Starbucks, not the country club.

If you're an old-style manager, you have to make adjustments here. You have to be prepared for the unexpected. For the fact that your sense of patterns and places may be far different from that of your dot-com colleagues. Let me give you a little test. How would you have reacted if this had happened to you?

I arrived at a dot-com office one morning for a meeting. I was running late, a concept that, by the way, is not recognized in the dot-com world. People don't "run late." They have alternate plans. And alternate plans means that no one ever apologizes for hanging you up.

On the conference table in the meeting room that morning was my meeting date, legs crossed, arms folded, head back. That's right, ON the table. Not at it. He was rocking back and forth, humming in a low voice.

"You're sitting on that *Wall Street Journal,*" I said, annoyed that anyone would be so presumptuous as to make themselves so comfortable in a space that was clearly and by design meant for one specific purpose. And it wasn't yoga. "You'll get much more out of it if you read it."

My guest did not move. "You've got bad karma, dude. Chill. Listen to what your body is telling you."

"I know what my body's telling me, thanks very much. It's telling me that it's time for a meeting and you're in the way. And it's also telling me that if you don't move on your own, I will move you."

My young colleague opened his eyes. "Aggression, man. Too much aggression."

He was right. There is a distinct lack of aggression in the dot-com world. There is also a distinct lack of convention. I mean, really. When was the last time you walked into a meeting room at your office at the bank and found someone practicing yoga or whatever on your table? And when you complained, you were the one who had the problem.

If you are anywhere within a fifty-mile radius of being a Corporate Toady, get ready to open your mind. Look at things a little differently. That concept of a place for everything and everything in its place? Forget it. Nothing is where it should be in dot-comland. Not the ideas, not the furniture, not the people.

If you are a Dot-Com Dynamo and find all this chat about nap rooms to be tiresome, what else can I say but sleep tight.

chapter eight

On Technology

W hen something breaks at home, like a toilet or a furnace, you call in an expert to fix it, right? A no-brainer. These are essential parts of the physical plant that cannot afford to be handled by an amateur.

Still, when the expert comes, you watch him work trying to figure out how he does what he does so that maybe, next time, you might attempt to fix it yourself and buy a small imported sedan with the savings. When he's done, you ask him what was wrong. If it's a toilet, it usually has something to do with valves, flanges, or floats. If it's a furnace, we're talkin' pumps, thermostats, and pilot lights.

You need this information. It is critical to the reinforcement of your role as Lord of the Manor, knower of all things masculine and machine-like. Really, you need to know it so that when your wife asks you what was wrong, you have an answer.

"Nothing serious, honey," you say, with just the hint of a western drawl. "The triradial hydroinverter relay got stuck on the tertiary flange mechanism. Happens all the time on these GTX-3000 models."

She knows you have no idea what you're talking about. And you know that she knows that you have no idea what you're talking about. But she nods, expresses her gratitude with a pat on the head. At least she didn't have to waste her

— ◆ —

...The triradial hydroinverter relay got stuck on the tertiary flange mechanism ...

— ◆ —

time overseeing some sweaty, smelly warthog of a service man with his belt hanging too low around his butt for polite company. You hike up your pants, dust off your hands, and reach for a beer. You are the conqueror. You have earned sustenance. You think for a moment about spitting, to mark your territory, but pull back. She would kill you if you messed up the carpet.

Getting a computer or other technological device fixed is really no different. They really require experts to do the job, no matter how simple the solution. Problem is, as with toilets and furnaces and other things mechanical, it is very difficult to decipher the explanation for the problem without an advanced degree in programming or tech support. It is for me, anyway.

I asked the young fellow who fixed my office desktop PC one day what was wrong with it. This is what he said. Or at least, this is what I think he said. I am certain this is what I heard:

> Pretty simple, really. The thrust inverter that downlinks to the rotors in System Q was exfoliated from the catalytic converter during the spin cycle. When this happens, the only way to restore the giga-function is to redirect processing through the distributor cap. Then bingo, the down-put and up-put are transmogrified, and the data is cauterized, catheterized, and martinized. You're all set.

Was I talking to the Reverend Jesse Jackson? I asked him to repeat the explanation, in layman's terms.

With a sigh, he said exactly the same thing, word for word. Only this time, he spoke more slowly and raised his voice. Like he was talking to someone for whom English was a second language. Come on, you've done it, too. Asking for directions in some foreign country. You think that the volume of the speaker is in direct relation to the comprehension of the listener. If you yell at the top of your lungs, "Where is the f——ing Coliseum?" they will know exactly what you want. They don't. I didn't either.

So, despite two explanations of the problem, I went home that day with no clue about what was wrong—not even a vague idea from which to formulate a standby statement. My wife, sensing my uneasiness, pounced.

"So, I tried to e-mail you today but couldn't get through.
What was wrong with your computer?"

"Nothing. Absolutely nothing. Must have been a
problem at your end."

I stuffed a meatball in my mouth, signaling to her that
the discussion was at an end. She understood. And I knew
that she understood. And she knew that I knew that she
understood. We ate dinner in silence.

— ◆ —

I asked a dot-com colleague how things were going. He had to consult his Palm Pilot to frame a reply.

— ◆ —

Such is life in the world of technology, which has per-
meated all economies, old and new. But I will say that in
the dot-com world, it is even more frightening, because the
technology is the heart and soul of the operation. And it
has spread far beyond the desktop. It's a jungle out there
for anyone who is the least bit squeamish about things
technological.

Here's what I mean. Ever go to a meeting where no
one could finish a sentence or even a subordinate clause
without some handheld device like a pager or a cell
phone or a Palm Pilot ringing, beeping, buzzing, chirp-
ing, or burping out a digital version of Beethoven's Fifth?

Worse, ever go to a movie or a restaurant where the same thing happens?

I asked a dot-com colleague the other day how things were going. He looked at his Palm VII and replied: "Stock. Down. Jenny. Birthday. Report. Late. Lunch. Pete's. Gym. Abs. Dinner. Eight."

I think that if his batteries had died he would have said: "Life. Over."

Things are getting so bad on this front that society is being split down the middle. There are those who are connected. And those who are not connected. Institutions are taking up sides. There is a restaurant in the Chelsea district of New York City called Vox that claims to be the first dining establishment in the country to offer patrons a separate section for cell phone use while they are eating. The reviews of the restaurant claim that the feature was borne of the management's understanding that cell phone users prefer some privacy. But it is pretty clear that is a snow job. For any of you who have wanted to strangle someone at the next table whose phone chirps to life throughout dinner, and who then talks endlessly about his or her mundane life in a loud voice, you know exactly why this restaurant added this feature. Liability. It did not want to be responsible for cell-related homicides.

Some reactions are far plainer. At the coffee shop at the commuter train station where I get my morning jolt of caffeine, there is a sign of warning. It is written in poorly formed block letters, in black marker, on an odd-sized piece of cardboard. It is taped in a prominent place above the rack of bagels, so it is sure to be seen. It reads: "Cell phone use is NOT welcome at this counter." And they mean it. On several occasions I have seen the proprietor ask people to tune out conversations while on line.

If this kind of stuff drives you crazy, think twice about working at a dot-com. Not only because that's what meetings are like there, but also because you really do need to know how to use all those things to keep up. It's all about connectivity. Either you're in or you're out. It's pretty simple.

We talked elsewhere about connectivity as it relates to the changing concept of time in the Internet space, because that is an important factor to consider. But right now we need to talk about the behavioral change you have to go through to attempt what is called "multitasking," a fancy word for doing all sorts of stuff at once and still being effective at each task. Because multitasking is at the heart of the connectivity revolution, which in turn is at the heart of the technological revolution. Don't even bother buying all the devices if you can't multitask. It will be a waste of money.

Changing behavior on this front means you have to go way back, to your childhood. Remember when your mom said, don't run with scissors? Turn off your music while you do your homework? Don't read and watch TV at the same time—you'll never learn anything? Don't talk to someone else while you're talking on the phone, too? It even applied to career advice: Pick one thing you're good at and do it as best you can.

Those of us of a certain age have been trained since childhood to do one thing at a time, to avoid distractions from the task at hand. In effect, to single-task. Consecutive, not concurrent. One after the other, not all at once. Well, forget about that idea. Strike it from your memory. Cleanse yourself of such archaic thoughts.

Actually, modern commerce will do it for you. It's actually been doing it for years. You may have simply been too busy adjusting to realize that you were actually adjusting.

Because as well as single-tasking worked, it was limited in scope and, many believed, didn't allow us humanoid carbon-based units to live up to our potential. On average, we only used 10 percent of our brains—some less, few more—so there was lots of room for improvement. So along came things like conference calls, where a bunch of people talked at once. That wasn't right, in the old sense, but since it was considered to be more efficient, it stuck. Then came the teleconference, because someone figured that it was important to see the people who were talking, as well as to hear what they said. Why, I'm not sure. Perhaps because with all this technology, our attention and comprehension had become so deadened that we needed to see people's lips moving to understand what they meant.

To me teleconferencing is like eating at a rural luncheonette. I really don't need or want to see whoever it is serving up the grub. I just want to eat it and get out of there.

Anyway, after the conference calls and the teleconferences came the fax and the PC and the printer, and pretty soon, our desks got pretty crowded. And we had all sorts of new ways to communicate and be communicated with. And we learned that it was not only acceptable to talk on the phone while sending e-mail (though I still yell at people who do this because I think it's discourteous) but that it was encouraged as a way to make maximum use of time as well. It made us more efficient, more useful. Forget about taking time to think. A quick response was all that mattered.

The time it took for someone to "get back to you on that" was condensed even further.

Thank God we still had the quiet times that came with our commutes to and from the office each day. And the sanctuary of our homes, our gardens, our barstools.

Well, that didn't last either. PCs flooded the "home market." And cell phones and pagers made us reachable anytime, anywhere. But reachable isn't exactly the same as productive, so along came things like handheld computing devices—Palms and Blackberries—which allowed us to write, e-mail, check stocks, shop, do all the things we need to do, but to do them while we were doing other stuff.

And that's pretty much where we are today. Connected. Not just reachable, but productive and efficient, too.

If you think that walking and chewing gum is multi-tasking you are probably a Corporate Toady. That has been one of the benchmarks of dexterity. Like rubbing your stomach and patting your head. Or is it patting your stomach and rubbing your head? Either way, if you consider these simple tasks concurrently, you have a lot of work to do. You need to learn what each mobile device does. You need to learn to distinguish the beeps. Like bird-watching for geeks. Then you need to be able to lead them like the conductor of an orchestra, making sure each one adds to the symphony in its own way so that the end product is a beautiful thing to behold.

Then, of course, you need to have a bag big enough to carry all this hardware, or have your tailor add a couple of pockets to your coat. Better yet, get a bunch of those little holsters that allow you to carry all your devices on your belt. It's very cool. And if you put them all on vibrate mode, you can massage the muscles in your lower back at the same time. Believe me, they'll need it.

If you are even less multitask-oriented than that—if your idea of multitasking is sitting and chewing gum at the same time—give up now. There is no hope for you. I have a fountain pen I can send to you. Better yet, have someone order it for you on eBay.

—◆—

Working at a dot-com is all about connectivity. Either you're in or you're out.

—◆—

If you are one of the smart ones, you can talk and make sense at the same time. It's not really multitasking in the Internet sense of the word, but it is on the right track. If you can accomplish this, you have begun to master the real trick about connectivity. You understand that the missing ingredient in this rush to respond is thinking. Actually taking information, digesting it, analyzing, giving it context, forming an opinion and a point of view, and generating some sort of recommendation on what to do with it. It is a dying art form, this thinking. Dying mainly because to do it properly takes time. And who has time anymore? For anything?

The broader issue here is that efficiency for efficiency's sake is a dangerous road to take. Isn't it more important to be right than right now? If you think so, you can do wonders in dot-comland.

If you are one of these people who moves from device to device in fluid motion, using each to its capacity and actually linking them together in some sort of network that allows one device to answer another, without you ever having to become part of the mix, congratulations. Chances are, you are a Dot-com Dynamo. You can talk on the cell, check stock prices and shop for books on your Palm Pilot, send e-mails on your Blackberry, and leave text or voice messages on your digital pager. That satellite phone will allow you to talk directly to that chip manufacturer in Taipei, even if you're at dinner in Soho.

But you're even farther ahead of the curve. You're already thinking about what happens after what comes next. You've already placed an order for the chip that can be surgically implanted into your head so that you won't have to carry all these different devices.

Live long and prosper.

chapter nine

On Fashion

Forgive me for being presumptuous here. But I wanted to save you a lot of time and effort. And embarrassment.

And if you're from the Midwest or Florida or any other part of the country where bright colors are acceptable forms of self-expression, pay particular attention. The color of choice in the dot-com world is black. Not charcoal or gunmetal gray. Not black mixed with anything else, like Black Watch tartan plaid. It's good old jet black. Witch's hat black. Texas tea.

Trust me on this one. This is not a race thing. It is a style thing.

If you're a woman, you know this is really a good thing. Every designer in the world will tell you that dark colors are slimming. And black, being by definition the ultimate absence of light, is the most slimming of all.

Think of all the aggravation you will save. Remember when you used to get your "colors" done? Forget it. Black goes with everything, and everything goes with black.

Of course, in the dot-com world, nothing accents black like, well, more black. So it is ridiculously easy to pick accessories for outfits. Here's my fashion guide:

Outfit: Black dress
Accessories: Black shoes, handbag, belt, and scarf

Outfit: Black pantsuit
Accessories: Same as above

Outfit: Black skirt and sweater
Accessories: Same as above

See how easy? That's about all you need to know. Oh, except for sunglasses. They must be black. And they must be worn at all times, rain or shine, day and night, all year long. This is important. I'm not sure why, but it is. You'll just have to believe me.

If you're a man and you skipped over the last few paragraphs, go back now and read from the top. This stuff applies to you, too. In fact, it probably applies to you even more. Especially the part about black being slimming. If you're a middle-aged man who has spent his career behind a desk, chances are your experience isn't the only thing that's expanded over time. Even if you go to the gym regularly, time and biology are taking their toll, and no doubt they will continue to do so.

Here's my fashion guide for you:

Outfit: Black shirt and pants
Accessories: Black belt, socks, and shoes

That's about all you need to know, except where to get acceptable versions of these articles of clothing, which we will discuss in another chapter. See how simple.

— ◆ —

Think Stalin.

Che Guevara.

Lucifer.

— ◆ —

After a few months, you may want to experiment. Kick it up a notch. Replace the black shirt with a black turtleneck. And the black shoes? Try something with a buckle. But be careful. If your neck is bigger than sixteen-and-a-half inches, a turtleneck will make you look like the top end of a bleach bottle. And if the buckles on the shoes are too garish, you will look like a pirate. And no matter how tempting, you do not want to be on the slippery slope toward an eye patch.

While we're here, let's talk for a minute about facial hair. It is not only acceptable (for men) but also encouraged. But beware. Don't go overboard. Full bushy beards are out. The dot-com world is no place for someone who looks like Grizzly Adams or a member of the Swedish parliament.

Think Stalin. Che Guevara. Lucifer. Remember, the more ways you can emulate revolutionaries, the better off you are.

Of course, this is dangerous ground for men over a certain age. There is nothing quite so pitiful as a forty-year-old guy with a jazz patch and sideburns, unless of course he is actually a professional saxophonist. Also, if you have a tendency to beef up, as you probably have from years of sitting behind a desk, beware of any added facial shrubbery that will make your face look even fatter than it already is.

And a special note for bald men. Be painfully aware of the dichotomy of having more hair on the bottom of your head than on the top. I worked with a dot-com executive who was totally bald—I mean he was a chrome dome in the classic sense. Foolishly, and probably after one too many Jägermeisters with employees, he grew a beard. He was very proud of it. Said something about how it reaffirmed his virility.

Others weren't so kind. The reviews were less than charitable. Said one: "It looks like his head is on upside down." Ouch.

Appearing ridiculous is just one downside of this dot-com trend for men of a certain age. Your loved ones, comfortable and familiar with the clean-shaven you, may find facial hair repulsive. It is scratchy to the touch. It looks messy. It may have a negative impact on your sex life, if you still have one. If you don't, it may impede your ability to get one. Think carefully about this.

And another hint. If you're going to go this route, take care of your personal topiary. Wash it, trim it. Keep it neat and tidy. Remember, food and other stuff can get caught in it.

— ◆ —

Forget for a moment that your company has only enough cash to survive another fifteen minutes.

— ◆ —

Of course, if you are not old enough yet to cultivate a crop of convincing facial hair, don't despair. There are many products on the market that imitate real hair. Or try implants. They're expensive, but hell, your peak earning years are ahead of you. You know that new American Express card you got, secured with your stock option package? Give it a workout. You'll thank me.

Now, if you flipped ahead to this chapter just to find out what Bang Bang is, shame on you. There are many mysteries to the dot-com world, to be sure, but they will be revealed, all in good time.

First, you have to forget everything you've heard about what's important in the dot-com world. It's not about who's got the best technology, or the savviest management, or the strongest finances. It's not about offering the customer the best experience or attracting the best IT talent. Those things are important, sure. But the real battleground in dot-com is fashion. Forget for a minute that your company has only enough cash to survive another fifteen minutes. What you should be focused on is whether your butt looks fat in Lycra.

We talked about the fundamentals of dot-com fashion. If you don't look good in black, the Internet is not for you. It's a basic tenet of the electronic age. But then, who doesn't look good in black? In fact, some of the pudgy fortyish managers, male and female, I know would do themselves and everyone else a favor if they incorporated a little more of Satan's palate into their wardrobes.

It took me a while to learn this. After all, I came from very traditional work environments, fashionwise. My closet is full of navy blue and gray suits, white shirts, and rep ties that were the uniform of Wall Street. These ensembles are quite forgiving for those who may have seen their middles or rear ends expand with time and the inactivity that comes with more corporate responsibility. My collection of cuff links, including spectacular silver ones that spell out Tiffany in semaphore flag code, gather dust on my shelf.

Even my days as a journalist had certain formality, believe it or not. At the *New York Times*, editors were encouraged (a subtle, Timesian word for required) to wear ties at all times. Rather peculiar, I thought, for those of us who worked the late shift until two in the morning. For whom were we dressing, the thugs who would mug us on the subways going home?

Indeed, the traditional sense, as conveyed to me once by a former Wall Street boss, that "casual dress means casual thinking" is not valid in e-commerce. Rather, there is the notion that casual dress inspires creative thinking, that the shedding of corporate uniforms such as blue suits is key to Internet success. It is freeing, emancipating, unlocking some hidden juices that have been gurgling around inside the best managers for years but have somehow failed to flow out, perhaps because the Windsor knots were a little too tight.

The problem is, and let's be honest about this, most men over forty look bad in casual clothes. And I'm not talking about sweat pants or other forgiving loose-fitting clothes. I mean jeans, in particular, but even khaki pants and golf shirts, which were the weekend warrior's standard, but which have now crept from the yacht club to the office. Unless you are built like Jean-Claude Van Damme, you really should not be seen wearing casual clothes by anyone other than your family (assuming, as I do, that they love you no matter what), and certainly not in public. I am not kidding about this.

Which brings me to Dockers. A fatal mistake. Really. Forget about Dockers, guys. They don't count. A nice pair of Dockers casual slacks, full-cut for those expanding hips, are as bad as a Barney's suit on the dot-com chic scale. A comfortable, generously cut Brooks Brothers shirt? Tent-like, compared with the ultraslim, terminally synthetic tops in vogue in the Valleys. (And by the way, it is acceptable in dot-comland to refer to men's shirts as "tops" and to their clothing ensembles as "outfits." I told you this was scary.) Topsiders, loafers, wingtips? In a word, yuk. Anyway, should you be so foolish as to think that the casual dress that was acceptable on Fridays at IBM or the country club on weekends is acceptable in the dot-com world, think again. You will stick out like a sore thumb. They will snicker at you from the company Foosball table, trash you on the climbing wall. In the nap room, your blankie will be set apart from the others.

Here's the problem: finding hip clothes that fit. (We'll get to the discussion about hip clothes that are actually flattering in a minute.) Chastened after having been ostracized by my dot-com colleagues for wearing an Oxford button-down shirt and pair of khaki pants to the office—I thought they were inoffensive at the least and rather sporty at the best—I wandered into a Banana Republic store in Manhattan looking to upgrade or downgrade my wardrobe. I found a snake-hipped young clerk, appropriately androgynous, who looked nonthreatening to me, and asked if he (or was it she?) could show me some pants and shirts that might be acceptable for workdays at a dot-com company.

"Sure, hon," it said, "what size?"

My pants ranged in waist size from 38 to 40, depending on the cut and whether or not I had been to the gym that week. The length was steady at 32, my visits to the gym having no effect on my height, alas. Shirt sizes were pretty standard: 16 to 16½ neck, 34 or 35 sleeve, again depending on the cut.

I might as well have been speaking Greek when I relayed this information to my young helper.

"I don't think we have pants THAT big," it said, raising the volume of the statement near the end. "I'll look in the back. You can check the rack to see if there's an odd size that slipped out. As for shirts, we have large, medium, small, and extra small. That's it."

And with that, it turned on its well-shod heel and scampered into the back of the store in search of giants' clothing, clucking all the way about carbohydrate addictions and ab crunches.

Undaunted, I looked through the pant rack nearby. Sure enough, the waist sizes stopped at 36 on the upside, and went down to 24 at the low size. I mean, I think my waist was bigger than 24 inches at birth. I looked around to double-check that I wasn't in the women's section. I was disappointed. I picked up the 36-incher and held it in front of me. Not even in my wildest dreams, where I am Patrick Swayze's stunt double, could I have fit into those pants.

— ◆ —

It turned on its well-shod heel and scampered into the back of the store in search of giants' clothing.

— ◆ —

But hope was not lost. My faithful but bemused clerk/friend emerged from the back room beaming, holding a pair of pants aloft and smiling. It began its remarks well before it reached me, ensuring that most others in the store could hear what it was saying.

"I found a pair of 38s," it puffed. "Must have been sent to us by mistake . . . these sizes usually go to the Midwest."

Ouch, I thought. I smiled appreciatively, nonetheless. I was embarrassed but relieved. Perhaps there was hope for me. He handed the pants to me, and directed me to a changing room. As I walked proudly toward the room, I noticed that the tag on the pants said Waist: 38, Leg: 35. Quick calculations told me that the person meant to wear these pants was probably four or five inches taller than me and considerably slimmer. I also figured that on my frame, the crotch of the pants would settle somewhere around my knees, making walking difficult, without shredding the material.

I mentioned this design flaw to my helper. "This is your only shot," it said, and turned away.

— ◆ —

Do you remember

the leisure suit?

— ◆ —

You can pretty much anticipate the outcome. The pants were cut so thin through the hips that I could not even get them on above my thighs. I hopped and jumped and sucked in every part of my body but to no avail. I knew then the meaning of my father's somewhat cryptic comment, "There's a reason sausages have a stretchy skin. Otherwise, they'd just be chopped pork." (Of course, he was one of the few people slim enough to actually look good in seersucker.) I stopped the struggle and admitted defeat.

Emerging from the dressing room, I noticed the concerned look on the clerk's face. Perhaps he had heard my grunts and groans as I tried to stuff myself into the pants, and was worried I might expire right then and there. The expression on his face was not so much one of compassion as it was relief that he wouldn't have to clean up the mess if

I croaked on his shift. I left the store empty-handed, except for the bagfull of disappointment that weighed on my shoulders.

My next stop, a store on Eighth Avenue called Bang Bang. That's no typo, my friends. Bang Bang. I could only imagine what the name meant but was afraid to let my mind wander there. It didn't matter, really. I was getting desperate. And here, at Bang Bang, I was assured by those who knew about such things, I was to find an oasis of dot-com-approved apparel.

Before I go further, let me ask a question. Do you remember the leisure suit? I mean, how could you forget, right? O.K., now keep the leisure suit image in your mind, eliminate the pastel polyester composition, and replace it with a texture, like leather. Or plastic. Better still, rubber. That's pretty much what you get at Bang Bang. Leather, plastic, or rubber leisure suits. "Accented with a rich mauve top and you're all set for that big meeting," advised Marc, my "fashion associate" that day. I waited until I was back out on the sidewalk before I wept.

For women, it's no different. Don't be caught dead in couture. Did you ever think you'd be telling yourself this? Ann Taylor is for PTA meetings. T.J. Maxx is for, well, do you remember my clerk's comment about the Midwest?

Androgynous is in. Bang Bang is the source. There is an upside, though. If you're wearing a rubber leisure suit, you really don't have to go home to change before you go out clubbing. Makes it a little easier to take, doesn't it?

Now any discussion about dot-com fashion is incomplete without a special focus on pajamas. In the dot-com world, pajamas are more than just clothing. They are a style staple. It is not uncommon to see men or women wearing pajama bottoms to work as if they were regular pants. They seem to be one of the few articles of clothing that are exempt from the "black preferred" rule. And woven into that paisley-patterned sleepwear are symbols of so much that is at the heart of dot-com: creativity, individuality, comfort. And rebellion.

And before you think that pajamas are limited to the workplace for Dot-com Dynamos, let me make this clear: Pajamas, particularly the bottoms, are perfectly acceptable wear for after-work activities, business lunches or dinners, or evenings at the clubs. But let's not get carried away here and kid ourselves. Pajamas, and the fact that they are worn to work without repercussions, mean that they are a big "screw you" to the old economy. To authority. To hierarchy. To convention and tradition. They say, loud and clear, that you don't need a suit-and-tie uniform to be important, successful, or rich.

Now don't get me wrong. I'm not suggesting that it isn't high time someone gave the stiff middle finger to all that corporate baloney and those who have been serving it up for so long. And frankly, I couldn't have come up with a more appropriate vehicle than pajamas. I will be the first to admit that when I used to wear pajamas, I wore them only to sleep in. They were not really to be seen outside of bed. I mean, that's why they invented bathrobes. So, bravo for letting your imagination run wild.

Funny thing, though. In a strange way, while nobody was looking, pajamas have become uniforms in themselves. They have spawned the casual sloppiness that has become the norm in the dot-com world. Conformity, unfortunately, is comforting, even for rebels. It's human nature, the need to fit in somewhere. And the more chaotic the environment, the greater that need.

But don't feel too bad. It happens all the time. Remember when blue jeans were the rebel uniform? Hip hugging, all natural, priced for the masses. Forget for a moment that cowboys were the authentic users of jeans, which have a design and durability that are useful for a life of punchin' doggies. Every trend has to start somewhere, so why not the Wild West?

— ◆ —

I will be the first to admit that when I used to wear pajamas, I wore them to sleep in.

— ◆ —

Anyway, eventually, everyone started wearing jeans, including the Establishment types who were the rebels' enemy. (And the many reasons why Establishment types shouldn't wear jeans are addressed elsewhere in this chapter. If you missed it, the subject falls into the same category as why men over thirty shouldn't go shirtless, even in their own homes.) So when it appeared that their uniform was being adopted by the other side, the rebels started modifying jeans to set them apart even more and make them their own once again. They ripped them; they stained them; they added patches and embroidery. They stone-washed them. But the masses followed, too.

Eventually, the fashion designers jumped in. In fact, a true low point in the development of modern civilization was the day Sergio Valente jeans hit the stores, and people of all shapes and sizes started shoe-horning themselves into the pants with the gold bull horns on the back pockets. Am I right about this? O.K., you purists probably think that a close second is the day "loose-fit" and "relaxed-fit" jeans hit the market at stores like the Gap and Banana Republic. And every suburban weenie in the country bought a pair and strutted around the mall thinking that he looked like Steve McQueen. I'll give you that one.

The point is, pajamas, or pajama-like work clothes have gone mainstream in the dot-com world. And with that has gone many of the powers of insurgency. Like I said, the quest for conformity, even in a chaotic environment, is human nature.

Maybe this is all an indication that the dot-com world is maturing. That a real society is emerging out of the hype and hysteria of the early years of development. That the abnormal is becoming normal. The unacceptable is becoming acceptable.

Or maybe I'm reading way too much into the "Dr. Denton Syndrome." Maybe all this means is that it's time to find another symbol of the revolution. A new icon to capture the imagination of the faithful.

I don't know much, but I think it might be profits.

chapter ten

On Harassment

Guys often talk about how confusing the world is. Especially when it comes to understanding women, and how to treat them. Women of course think understanding them is easy, and that guys are confused simply because they don't listen. At least I think that's what they think. I wasn't paying close enough attention. But the point is that the relationship between men and women has been forever altered by the workplace, the changing roles it has created, and the peculiar dynamics it has fostered between the sexes.

I'm no expert on this topic. But I am a man who for more than twenty years has been trying to figure out how to navigate a safe yet effective course through the workplace in an era when the dynamic tension between men and women in the work environment has come to a head.

And I will be the first to admit that while much of the sexual harassment stuff is pretty easy to fathom, other parts of it are not quite so clear.

Here's an example of the former. I was managing a department at a newspaper and a young woman reporter came to me one day with a complaint. Apparently a co-worker, a man, had approached her at a private party one night and taken her photograph with a portable, instamatic camera. It seemed innocent enough at the time. She really thought nothing much of it then, because he was taking pictures of many people at the party, and in fact several other people were also photographing the activity. It was, after all, a party.

But it didn't stop there. It turned out that over a period of months, the shutterbug was taking photographs of this woman reporter as she arrived at work, left work, even while she was sitting at her desk. No one knew this guy's proclivities until one day, inadvertently, she was walking by his desk in the newsroom and noticed that among the photos and notes on his bulletin board was a photo of her. It was not taken at the party in question, and in fact she couldn't figure out where it was taken or when. She was a little taken aback. But she tried to laugh it off.

"That's not a very good picture of me, is it?" she said. "I look awful." She told me later that she hoped her tone and self-criticism would convince him to take down the photo.

But rather than take the hint, he surprised her again, and even more so. He reached into his desk drawer and pulled out an envelope.

"Well, if you don't like that one, I've got a bunch more to choose from," he said, digging inside the envelope and extracting a dozen more snapshots of her taken at various times in various places. "Help me pick one."

She was mortified. She was frightened. It was clearly a situation that went beyond the normal bounds of acceptable behavior, especially in the workplace. We took the complaint through the process, and the sicko was fired.

Like I said, a fairly easy case in which to determine right from wrong. No confusion, no gray area.

But here's where it can get complicated. And I know I'm not alone on this. There are a lot of guys who went through the sexual harassment era of the 1980s and 1990s who are still not sure whether they should ever open another door for a woman or not.

When I was a kid, I was taught basic common courtesy. Open doors for people. Look people in the eye when they speak to you. Don't interrupt. All that stuff. A subset of that was all about the things to do for or say to women. If my sister was going to a party, and she was dressed up, my mother would tell my brother and me, "Tell your sister she looks nice." And we would. We would also hold doors for women, help them with their coats, walk on the outside of them while on sidewalks. Later on, we would hold chairs for them at tables, light their cigarettes, and make other small gestures that were considered gentlemanly behavior.

It's not like we were freaks, though today people think it's remarkable if any of those niceties are performed. I mean, Cary Grant did it, James Bond did it. Any role model worth his salt was well versed in the gentleman's etiquette.

Now I have no intention here of picking a fight with anyone who thinks such behavior is degrading to women or a reinforcement of the weaker sex label. That it is not so much courtesy and respect as pandering and phony solicitousness. Personally, I think that argument is drivel. My point is that for men of a certain age or training, that sort of thing was accepted behavior, indeed required behavior. It was not abnormal or aberrant. It was not harassing or threatening.

Despite the free-for-all of the dot-com world, when it comes to gender issues, things have not changed much.

Now, granted, as I said, the workplace changed many of the dynamics, and many people, both men and women, had trouble keeping their hands to themselves, no matter what their training. But for those of us who were genuinely trying to figure out how to separate proper behavior as we knew it from acceptable behavior as determined by law, it was an interesting experience. Common sense, or rather common courtesy, was not always the safe and sure route.

I am sad to say that despite the free-for-all of the dot-com world, things have not changed much. They have certainly not changed for the better. Which is a little surprising, because of the casual nature of the environment and the relationships that flourish therein. I suppose that no matter what the environment, the changing relationships between men and women in the workplace will continue to be a source of confusion.

Anyway, personal appearance and one's desire to comment on it remain touchy subjects in dot-comland. So be careful. If you're a traditionally trained manager who has been through the wars of sexual harassment in the workplace, you are only half prepared for what awaits you. All that stuff about no touching, no tickling, no tongues. All very valuable, indeed. But this is not about sexual harassment at all. It's about what I call the "hip deficit." It afflicts old-economy managers. It is the nemesis of the Corporate Toady.

Now, as long as you Toadies stay where you are, in that homogeneous old-world economy that approximates the suburbs, this will never be a problem. Sort of like having toenail fungus and never taking off your socks in public. But when you enter the dot-com world, you are exposed. It can cause more than embarrassment. It can tar you for good as a weenie. And you will never, ever get anyone from the Help Desk to fix your computer, no matter how important you are or how urgent your need.

If you are over forty, you cannot cure the "hip deficit." Unless your name is Mick Jagger. I'm afraid the condition is terminal. You can shop at all the right stores. You can wear nothing but black. You can get your hair cut like a Roman emperor, have a tattoo of Jeff Bezos on your forearm, and install a nipple ring made from a Pentium chip. It doesn't matter. Trust me on this.

But you can live a normal and healthy life if you follow this simple guideline:

Never, ever comment on anyone's appearance, even if you think it's a compliment.

And I mean never. Not even an indirect reference, like "You know, George Clooney looks good in plaid, too." Not even a gesture or a glance. Nothing. Nada. Nyet.

The day I learned I had "hip deficit" was a low point in my professional life. How was I to know? No one told me. I learned the hard way, on my first Halloween in Silicon Alley. Many of my dot-com colleagues wore costumes to

— ◆ —

If you are over forty, you cannot cure the "hip deficit," not even if you install a nipple ring made from a Pentium chip.

— ◆ —

work that day. And I mean these people went crazy dressing up. They were creative to the extreme, and they executed down to every detail. They clearly were not afraid to spend some of their hard-earned money to excel in fantasy. It was truly breathtaking.

On my way to get coffee in the company cafeteria, I bumped into a woman who looked spectacular. Big orange hair. Black lipstick and nail polish. This really frightening, witchy, lace dress, with elbow-length lace gloves. Black high-heel boots that laced up the front. She was Morticia Addams and Lily Munster combined, and come back to life. I couldn't contain myself.

"That is a great costume," I gushed. "You look terrific."

She looked at me. (And you probably know where this is going, don't you?) She looked at me like I was a fat forty-something who wouldn't know hip if he fell over it.

"What are you talking about?" she snorted. "What costume?"

Boy, was my face red. I was busted. Living, shaking proof that no good deed goes unpunished.

If you are a Corporate Toady or even a Closet Creative, don't make the same mistake. You are in the conventional group that may be a little skeptical of the freedom of expression that is the norm in the dot-com. Body piercings upset you, not simply because they are unfamiliar fashion-wise, but they also look painful. You believe there are only two real hair colors—blond and brunette—because those are the only colors you would ever consider for yourself. (And you have been one or the other, too, at certain points in your life.) Anything else is, well, weird. But bite your tongue if you have to, rather than blurting out your opinions on this stuff. Smile if you can. Otherwise, just look away.

(Now you redheads may be wondering why you have been left out. Au contraire. You are a special group. Not to worry. The rules don't apply to you. Make fun of anyone you want. Everyone is afraid of you anyway. They think you're crazy. Like in medieval times, when redheads were considered witches. It hasn't changed much. So have a blast.)

If you're like my witchy woman colleague, you're probably used to taking heat for your nonconformity. At home. At school. At the human sacrifices in the company cafeteria at the lunch hour. Ignore the critics. They're the ones with the problem. And if you seek revenge, lawsuits are for wimps. Harassment suits are even worse. He said. She said. Be more direct. Inflict bodily harm. Change the dynamic to, "I said it all and he said nothing."

— ◆ —

I smiled meekly, hoping she wouldn't recognize me without my foot in my mouth.

— ◆ —

If you're under thirty and your definition of hip includes no hair at all, congratulations. Shaved heads are cool, as long as you're not part of some neo-Nazi group. It's hard to raise venture capital money if that kind of thing gets around. But hey, no one gives Governor Jesse the Body Ventura any flack for his dome anymore.

If you're over forty and you have no hair, my condolences. It is very difficult to disguise your affliction as hip. You are fooling no one. O.K., if you want to perpetuate the myth that bald men are smarter and more virile than their hairy counterparts, that's fine with me. I know. Grass doesn't grow on a busy street. Whatever kind of rationalization helps you make it through the night.

Now, maybe I'm being a little too hard on the old-economy managers. I mean, "hip deficit" is an affliction, like listening to Yes. But the dot-com youngsters aren't above a little treachery, either. In fact, dot-com harassment can work in reverse.

Not long after my Halloween encounter, I wore a suit to work because I was having dinner with an old-economy friend. I was pleased to have the opportunity to dress up again, if only for the occasion. The crisp starched white shirt, the shiny shoes, the collar stays, and the cuff links. When you think about it, it is a pretty kooky get-up, especially for everyday use. But I wore it proudly that day, and I put up with the usual jokes at the office about having a job interview or a funeral.

At one point, I slipped into the kitchen to get coffee. Believe it or not, there was Morticia making some sort of herbal tea from Tibet. I smiled meekly, hoping she wouldn't recognize me without my foot in my mouth. No such luck.

"You're all dressed up," she said, sneering.

I stopped and looked at her. Was she setting me up? I didn't care. What was that they say about vengeance being a dish best served cold?

"What do you mean?" I replied. "I often wear a suit and tie to work. Because I like to. I'm not dressed up."

I couldn't tell whether she had planned the exchange just to stick it to me or if she really didn't realize what she had done until after the fact. But I do know this. She wasn't lying the first time when she said the witch get-up wasn't a costume. I know, because since then, she has made the company's market capitalization disappear.

chapter eleven

On Keeping Current

I will admit this right up front: I am a news junkie. More specifically, I am a newspaper junkie. I love the smell of them, the feel of them. I love every antique, archaic, prehistoric wrinkle of them. I love them with coffee in the morning, on the train to work, in an easy chair on a winter Sunday afternoon.

I have yet to cultivate the same intimate relationship with my television, PC, laptop, or Palm VII, though each of them also offers me the news of the day.

This shouldn't surprise you. I am the son of a newspaperman. I am the brother of a newspaperman. I am a newspaperman. Or I was, until a few years ago. But I put in my time in the business, starting back at the dinner table when I was a kid, when we talked about the top stories of the day. What they meant. What the angle was. Where the twist lay.

It didn't matter what the story was about—sports, politics, crime, the weather. It was the craft that mattered as much as the subject itself.

And the same questions ended the discussion about each story: Do you believe it really happened the way they say it did? Do you trust the sources?

When I was a consultant, advising corporate executives about getting their companies' stories out effectively, I would counsel them on the credibility of various news outlets. The sources through which people got the news had a huge impact on the credibility of the story being told. The outlets had to be chosen carefully, to obtain maximum lift for the company.

During one of these counseling sessions, a senior executive asked me: "How do you know which outlets are credible?" It was a fair question, and one easily answered. There was no mystery to it, really. I responded with a question of my own: "Which ones do you trust?" (Do you see how easy it is to be a consultant? Get the clients to answer the questions themselves; then send them a bill for your services.)

He rattled off a list of the usual suspects: *The Wall Street Journal*; *The New York Times*; *Forbes*; *Fortune*; the major broadcast networks, including CNN; and on and on. He also named some trade publications that were of importance to his industry, and to the line managers who were engaged in the day-to-day management of the business. Exactly what you'd expect from a senior executive of a company looking for influential business coverage.

If he had been a professional athlete, his targets would have been different.

Had he been an artist, a musician, or a dancer, different still, in every way.

Now, it's not that the big well-known outlets didn't make mistakes. Reporters and editors are human, too, no matter what else you've been told. But it was pretty clear that if these outlets did make mistakes, they would correct

— ◆ —

You might even learn a thing or two about why your stock options wouldn't buy you a bus ticket back to Pittsburgh.

— ◆ —

them. They also took a lot of pains up front to get it right. And people knew that. And they trusted them as sources of news. And those were the criteria that this executive used when it came time to judge which outlets he considered to be worthy of cultivating.

Fast-forward to the dot-com world. In this environment, I would think twice about asking the same question: "Which outlets do you trust?" Here's why.

In the last ten years, the business and financial news media has exploded. The national obsession with investing in the stock markets has created a huge appetite for news about companies. The rise of dot-com companies has fueled the fire even more. Indeed, the dot-com companies were ready-made for this new generation of inexperienced investors who saw the markets as a game to be played. Many of these people had never seen a bear market. Many had never even seen a slowdown, or a correction, or a dip. They were babes in the woods, and the dot-coms were the big bad wolf.

When this new group of investors looked for information, increasingly they looked to the news media. It was plentiful, accessible, and free. Why bother getting a stockbroker to help me evaluate my long-term needs and objectives and tolerances for risks? Why bother paying for expensive research reports? I'll just watch CNBC and hear what Ron Insana has to say, or I'll log on to TheStreet.com and get James Cramer's latest hot stock tip. I can do my own research right from my Barcalounger and no one will know any better.

The problem is that like any business that grows so fast, the financial news business is suffering from a talent deficit. The need to fill acres of newsprint, hours of air time, and the bottomless pit of Internet pages has put a premium on getting warm bodies, any warm bodies, in the doors of news organizations to churn out content. The newsrooms of many of these new outlets are so green you could put Thousand Island dressing on them and eat them for lunch. How real is this deficit? Chances are that if you've got a pulse, you can get a job as a business reporter in this current market. If you don't have a pulse, you can be a political commentator. But that's another issue.

The downside of this talent deficit is obvious. All over the country, there are people with little or no training or experience calling themselves "journalists" and reporting on companies to an insatiable audience of individual investors. Not only that, they are being forced by the demand to offer opinion and insight, as well, not just facts. In effect, financial journalists have become amateur investment analysts, offering analysis and wisdom about the fundamentals of companies, their valuations, and the predicted movements of their stocks. And many individual investors base their decisions on what they believe is knowledge, when in fact it is drivel dressed up and expanded to fill time and space. The lack of oversight on this front has been conspicuous, yet it is the companies in question that bear the brunt of investors' complaints, even lawsuits, not the bearers of the advice. Don't shoot the messenger still seems to hold water in the financial news business, unlike in other parts of the news media.

And I'm not even talking here about the frauds who have taken to putting out fake press releases in an effort to move stock prices. That has happened more often than to constitute just isolated incidents. The phony releases have been picked up and circulated quickly by news organizations, so eager to get the story first that they did not care about getting it right. The lesson here is ridiculously basic: A seasoned reporter would know enough to call a company to check on the legitimacy of a release before running a story about it. Sounds simple, doesn't it? And it is, unless you don't know what you're doing.

At the same time, this intense competition to feed this broad new audience has pushed news organizations, particularly television outlets, to make business news more entertaining. Information isn't enough any more. It must be flashy, fun, exciting. Breathless anchors and reporters dominate the landscape, their big hair and big teeth standing out as credentials far more than the ability to read a balance sheet.

Internet newswires, too, are strained under the crush. Some have taken technological efficiency to absurd heights, installing computer programs that post stories to the Web automatically after a certain period of time, whether they have been edited and fact-checked or not. What are they thinking? That's what happens when the techies, not the journalists, run the newsroom.

— ◆ —

Chances are that if you've got a pulse, you can get a job as a business reporter in the current market.

— ◆ —

And if you want to get even deeper into the question of what sources you can trust, consider the new breed of journalist/investment adviser, like James Cramer. A prolific writer and skilled speaker, Cramer founded and funded TheStreet.com, one of the first online newswires to make a name for itself. He has come under fire from some conventional news media for what they say is conflict of interest for running a business about which he writes as a journalist. Yet he continues to write, own, and promote his ventures on television, in print, and online. The fact that his methods have not offended those who consume his extraordinary output of information and opinion on a regular basis says much about the tolerances and sensitivities of audiences in this new environment. Cramer's viewers and readers apparently care less about any ethical tightrope walking he may do than about the usefulness of the information he provides. In a world hungry for information, Cramer's frequent appearances on television and in print seem to be enough of a stamp of credibility to keep his faithful coming back for more.

You think I'm just a cranky old print journalist raging against the machine, don't you? That just because I put in more than fifteen years working my way up the ladder of journalism that somehow my view of what's right and true is somehow better than that of others. But I am not making this up. Stephen Ross, a Columbia University professor who studies the media, said this about his findings in a recent study of the online news media: "Journalists often got the story wrong . . . and skirted long-standing ethical practices concerning privacy and sourcing."

Add to this the growth of Internet chat rooms and bulletin boards, where rumor and innuendo flow freely back and forth. Unsubstantiated yet unrefuted, this kind of speculation quickly turns from idle chatter to news. And once it is in the technology pipeline, it can spread around the world in a heartbeat. Misinformation is virtually impossible to retrieve and correct. And if it can be done, chances are it's too late. Someone, somewhere has already acted on the information.

The big problem here is this: No one seems to make the distinction anymore about the credibility of the sources of their news. A story on Inside.com, a gossipy Internet rumor rag, is given the same heft as a story in *The Wall*

Street Journal. A profile in *Business Week* has just as much impact as a segment on *Access Hollywood*, though the latter has a bigger audience.

A young dot-comer called me one day very excited about an opportunity she had found through a friend of hers at an online newswire. The reporter wanted to interview the CEO, to talk about the business strategy and the

—◆—

The ability to keep up with who is fathering Madonna's child this year is not something most recruiters consider a "core competency."

—◆—

market. The newswire was so insignificant that if the request had not come from a colleague, I would have declined it without a second thought. But I agreed to talk with the reporter, to prescreen the questions.

Do you remember an infamous interview that Bill Clinton did with a twenty-something host on MTV during his second presidential campaign? The host, eager to get the inside scoop on Mr. Clinton for her curious viewers, asked him about his musical preferences, his musical heroes.

The President rattled off a number of names. "I particularly like Thelonius Monk," he said.

The host crinkled up her button nose and frowned. "The Loneliest Monk? Who's that?"

Well, my interview with this reporter went pretty much the same way. Aside from the fact that her voice was smurf-like, and you pretty much needed to be a dog to hear her up in that frequency, it was clear that business was not her forte, despite the fact that, according to her e-mail signature, she was indeed a "business reporter."

Terms were a weakness right off the bat.

Cash flow: "Does that mean in or out?"

Market cap: "Keeps the rain off your head."

EBIDTA: "Gesundheit!"

Am I exaggerating? Maybe, but only a little. I suggested she brush up a little before we put her with a senior executive.

Was I being mean? Not at all. The danger here is that inaccurate reporting can seriously damage your company, especially if it is publicly traded. People make financial decisions based on what they read in the news media. And if bad information gets out there, and is transmitted around the world in this era of technological wonder, it is hard to get it back. By the time it's corrected, decisions have been made, actions have been taken. If Lady Smurf had confused margins with melons, we would have been in trouble. And so would anyone who acted on the information in her story.

Now we could argue that the reason it has come to this is that Americans have become less discriminating consumers of news. If that's true, that's a very bad sign. Or we could say that they have become so skeptical that they don't believe anything any media outlet says. That's bad news, too, especially if you're running a company that is looking to attract investors and convince them that your story is credible. And that's just about every dot-com company that exists today.

For all you Corporate Toadies, you are, for once, in the right. This is one case in which being old economy is actually a good thing. And being aggressively old economy, unbending, unwavering, and unforgiving is a great thing. You can do the dot-com world a big favor if, when you come over, you bring that old gray slab called *The Wall Street Journal* with you. While you're at it, bring along *The New York Times* and maybe the *Financial Times*. And keep bringing them with you into the office every day. Make reference to them in meetings. Ask people if they've read this story or that. And you know those handwritten notes you're going to start distributing to colleagues? Why not attach a clipping from the *Journal* or another old-line media outlet once in a while. Every little bit helps.

If you're a TV fan, that's O.K., too. Because as long as you dedicate at least a few minutes a day to the news, it counts as an effort to keep current. But remember this: There is a difference between CNN and *C.O.P.S.* Trust me, there is, though sometimes you have to watch carefully to see it.

Let me be clear about one thing here. *People* magazine is not a news source. It is a fine publication, to be sure, if you want to know who the sexiest people alive are. But don't make the mistake of confusing its purpose. If you're a Desperately Seeking Something, avoid making reference to it in business meetings. Do not under any circumstances bring it up in a job interview, even at a dot-com. Your ability to keep up with who is fathering Madonna's child this year is not something most recruiters consider to be a "core competency."

And if you are a Dot-Com Dynamo, and for whatever reason you eschew the old methods of devouring news, be careful in the fickle world of cyber news. The information that you are consuming is hardly credible. As long as you acknowledge that, understand it, and at least try to supplement your daily intake with some old-economy sources, things will be O.K. You may even learn a thing or two about why your stock options wouldn't buy you a bus ticket back to Pittsburgh.

chapter twelve

On Compensation

Ask a man about his sex life, and he will probably have no problem with telling you a story or two about his wins and losses. Same goes for a woman, and although she may be a little less graphic in her descriptions, she will be no less enthusiastic about sharing her tales. Now maybe I simply hang around with people of loose morals and lips to match, but in my experience, it usually takes very little effort to get even strangers talking about the sins of the flesh.

Now ask the same man and the same woman how much money they make, or how much money they have, and it's a different story. They will be shocked, horrified. "It's none of your business," they will say. And they will mutter something about you being the devil himself for asking. It is the surest way to end a friendship, or to ensure that one never begins in the first place.

What is it that makes talk of the bed perfectly acceptable but talk of the bank off limits?

It may be, as many would suggest, that money is truly
the root of all evil. If that is so, then I have a follow-up
point to make: that stock options are the flowers that
bloom from the demon seed. And I hate to say I told you
so, but I was skeptical of them long before the bottom fell
out of the Internet market.

— ◆ —

If money is the root

of all evil, stock options

are the flowers that bloom

from the demon seed.

— ◆ —

Not that I'm a financial genius. Far from it. But I am a
world-class chicken. And when I entered the dot-com
world, the fact that stock options had become the core of
compensation packages, not supplementary vehicles to
reward a job well done, scared me to death. They were illu-
sory, intangible, a little too fuzzy for an old-style manager
like me, who has trouble balancing his checkbook. And
most of the stock option plans were set up in vesting plans
that were several years older than the companies that were
offering them, and several years older than the dot-com
market itself. There were a lot of basic, logical inconsisten-
cies that didn't make sense to me.

Stock options were ballyhoo, and they hooked a lot of fish. Unfortunately, they also created a lot of unrealistic expectations for a lot of naïve people. And that specter continues to hang over the dot-com world like a rain cloud.

Now don't get me wrong. I still hold out hope for the bucketful of stock options sitting on my desk that are so far under water I can sometimes hear them laughing at me. (Or maybe the laughter is coming from the old-economy friends to whom I boasted about my option plan.) I'm the kind of person who sees the world as a glass half-full. But let me tell you, if I had a nickel for every dot-com stock option I hold right now, I'd be a happy man. O.K., I'd even take a penny, just so I could get rid of them. They're taking up space in my psyche.

Bitter? Me? Would my story be a little different if I had been able to cash out early and was now writing this while sipping champagne on the afterdeck of a 150-foot Feadship motor yacht in Monte Carlo harbor? Of course it would. But the point is, my story is way more relevant now for those of you who are considering a career in the dot-com world. Because the days of the big score are over. The advice those instant Internet millionaires can give you is useless. Their timing was perfect. Mine wasn't. Yours may be even worse. We just have to live with the new reality of the "new" new economy, painful as it may be, and move on.

Frankly, the lesson I learned provides a cautionary tale, as the Internet moves into the next phase of its development. I come from a long line of skeptics who are faithful to the adage that if it sounds too good to be true, it probably is. Part of it is my reporter training. We are professional skeptics. And it's not because of any malicious streak or other psychological disorder. The reason is simple. Since everyone has an angle, everyone's story is biased to his or her own advantage. That's why it's important to get input from all sides. Somewhere in the middle lies the truth, or as close to the truth as anyone can ever get.

The other part of it is my upbringing. My parents came from modest beginnings: Dad, the son of a pharmacist in a one-horse Illinois town; Mom, the daughter of a wheat farmer who lost everything in the dust bowl of the Depression and traveled the Canadian prairies by covered wagon in search of work, food, and shelter.

It was my father's connection with a big corporation later in his life that provided the financial security that gave my siblings and me so much opportunity. He was a salaried guy who saved some here and there, provided a good home, and led a good life. But we were a long way from rich. And no one in our house ever forgot the lessons of the leaner times. Be thankful for what you've got, we were taught. If you get greedy, you will get burned.

Add to all this my terrible head for finance, and I was scared to death of anything I couldn't use as legal tender any time I wanted. Shortsighted? You bet. Maybe I am from Missouri after all.

So skeptical was I about the stock option thing that whenever I negotiated the compensation segments of my contracts in the dot-com world, I refused to be wowed by the offer of lots of stock options at the expense of a fatter annual salary. I always tried to err on the side of caution, no matter how unfashionable that was. It was my nature, after all.

"I would rather have a bigger salary and fewer options," I told one recruiter, as we dined at a quaint Tuscan-style restaurant in New York City's Chelsea district, Internet heavies all around us. "Options really don't mean that much to me. They don't pay the mortgage."

Suddenly, the restaurant fell silent. I could feel all eyes upon me. I thought I heard one turtlenecked man with a Julius Caesar haircut mutter "old-economy heathen," but I wasn't sure. He could have just been asking for more bread. But it was true that I had given myself away as a throwback. I felt like I had a tail, and checked to make sure my opposable thumbs still worked.

My recruiter was shocked, too. "This is a chance for wealth creation. To own a piece of the pie. That's why everyone gets into this business."

For a moment, I thought of Gordon Gekko in the movie *Wall Street*, where he tells the young Bud Fox that someone making a few hundred thousand dollars a year is nothing, nobody. If you want to be a player, Gekko said, you need to create wealth. If you want the private jets and the house in the Hamptons. If you want the Park Avenue apartment and the blonde girlfriend who could afford the expensive plastic surgery to get rid of those fins. That stuff costs real money. You have to think big. Be ruthless. You'll never get rich working for The Man.

Of course, like Gordon Gekko, my lunch companion was right. Salaries are for chumps. They're old economy, old thinking. But for the average manager in the old economy, there was not much access to things like stock options or even stock purchasing plans that were fundamental to wealth creation. In most companies, such perks filtered down only so far into the management ranks. You had to be pretty far up the totem to be included.

So it was no surprise that everyone charged into the Internet space in search of the grail that was the stock option package. Options were available to pretty much everyone, even down into the administrative levels and, at some companies, into the ranks of the hourly workforce, too. It was great for morale and, in an era of high turnover, a great way to attract and retain talent. And besides, when there were no more options left to give away, they'd simply print more. No problem.

— ◆ —

What was a

secretary doing getting

20,000 stock options?

— ◆ —

The system was way out of whack. What was a secretary doing getting 20,000 stock options in a company? I can hear you Corporate Toadies asking that question right now. I can also hear you Dot-com Dynamos saying, why not, and what's wrong with that? That's what the Internet was all about. Equality. Access. If you contributed in your own way, no matter what way that was, why shouldn't you be entitled to some of the spoils?

Yep, in the early days, getting a fat stringer of options was like shooting fish in a barrel. For people at the beginnings of their careers, there was nothing to lose and everything to gain. If they had a job, with a salary that paid the rent and the bar bill, that was enough. The fact that they could get several thousand options that could appreciate many times over when a company went public, well, that was like having a lottery ticket.

For people later on in their careers, this was a chance to wrap it up early. Hit it big, cash in and retire at forty. It was not their fathers' workplace, that was for sure.

And for a few years, the stock option lottery paid off on a regular basis. Companies went public, their stocks rocketed, and everyone got rich. Salaries were beer money compared with what these options were bringing home.

Some people cashed in and checked out. One friend bought a sixty-foot sailboat and went cruising around the world. I hear from him once in a while, usually by postcard from some exotic port where the sun is warm, the beer is cold, and living is easy. He isn't bored at all, not working, as several of us suggested he would be after several months of goofing off. Another bought a vineyard in California, where he hosts all-expense-paid get-togethers for his working-stiff friends, partly to rub it in, and partly because he simply can afford to do it.

Others have done less predictable things with their Internet fortunes than check out of the rat race. Mark Cuban, the brains behind Broadcast.com, which was bought out by Yahoo!, lived out a lifelong dream and bought a professional sports team, the National Basketball Association's Dallas Mavericks. By the way, while he's in his early forties now, he was a multimillionaire by the time he was thirty-one. He had to work a few more years to make it into the Billionaire Boys Club.

Clearly, guys like Mark Cuban, my sailor friend, and the Internet vintner are the exceptions. They are in the small percentage of those who really struck gold on the Internet. But it's their stardom that created the buzz that started the stampede.

I hate to rain on everyone's parade, but that rush is over. No matter who you are, Corporate Toady or Dot-com Dynamo. The consolidation in the Internet economy is an equal opportunity de-employer. There are enough pink slips out there to fill the Canyon of Heroes next time the Yankees win the World Series.

That's the stark reality of the dot-com world today. Will it change? Probably. The dot-com companies that survive and come back will be stronger and more stable than their early phase brethren. Their stocks will recover, and rise. But the experts say it is unlikely we will see the next generation of dot-com companies go through the roller coaster of wild stock gyrations. One, because the market has changed, and two, because the companies have changed. Everyone has become more mature, less prone to the highs and lows that come from youthful, irrational exuberance. And that means the new Internet fortunes will be made slowly, and over time, not quickly and overnight. Just like in the old days.

So if you're interested in making the jump, especially if you have a long way to jump from an old-economy company, take that into consideration. There are a lot of opportunities in the "new" new economy, but don't fall into the stock option trap. Make them part of your package, for sure. There's no incentive to perform like the chance to own a piece of a going, growing concern. But keep things in perspective. Don't bet the farm on stock options. Keep your expectations low, and you will never be disappointed.

chapter thirteen

On Communicating

I have a colleague named Tom. He is a great guy. So great, in fact, that I have come to think of him as more than a colleague. He is a friend. And he becomes a better friend with every passing day. How do I know this? Because I believe that through our relationship, I have come to know more about him than I know about almost anyone else in the world.

I know that he is married with two kids. I know that he lives in New Jersey. I know that he is an avid bicycle rider, and that his favorite color is green. I know that he worries a lot about what his kids watch on television. I know that he has a master's degree in education and a dog whose flatulence is causing a great deal of domestic angst in his household. I know that his favorite movies are film noir mysteries, especially those with Linda

Fiorentino, but he doesn't go to the theater as often as he likes because he has periodontal problems and it hurts him to eat popcorn, which is a big part of the enjoyment of films. I know a lot more about him, but I think you get the idea.

By the same token, Tom knows a lot about me, probably more than any person in the world other than my mother, and she's had more than eighty years of experience. And I don't just mean the big stuff like my favorite music and the fact that I believe the Toronto Maple Leafs are actually the best hockey team in the universe, despite not having won a Stanley Cup in decades. Minor details. I mean the little stuff, too, like my belief that anyone who puts fruit in any sort of baked goods is a witch, and that I truly believe the Thermos™ is the smartest device ever created. I mean, how does it know when to keep the cold stuff cold and when to keep the hot stuff hot? There are no buttons to be pushed, no knobs to be turned to adjust the mechanism. It just knows. And Tom knows I know this.

Yep, you could say that Tom and I are best buds. Chums. Mates. Oh, did I mention that I have never met Tom? I forgot, didn't I?

Yes, that's the point of this little tale. I have never actually met Tom. In person, I mean. I write him roughly five thousand words a day by e-mail, and I trade a dozen or so voice mails with him, but I have never had any personal contact with him. Never shaken his hand. Never seen his face.

I can only imagine if I were called to testify on his behalf as a character witness:

"And how long have you known Tom, Mr. Carlson?"

"More than three years, your Honor."

"And would you describe him as a man of good character?"

"Oh, yes, your honor. Impeccable. Honest, upstanding, wholesome. Integrity personified."

"Very well. Just for the record, would you kindly point out Tom to the court, so that we may verify that this is the same Tom to whom you are referring?"

Gulp. I would be busted. I wouldn't know where to point. And Tom would probably go to jail.

But such is life in the world of the dot-com. If you're in a traditional office, and use things like e-mail and voice mail on a regular basis, take your current experience and multiply by a gazillion, and you've pretty much got what it's like in the Internet world.

Personal interaction is considered passé, old world. The prospect of meeting someone face-to-face is, well, grotesque. Do you think this might have anything to do with casual attitude toward fashion? I mean, if you knew you could get through the business day without seeing anyone, wouldn't you wear your pajamas to work? O.K., that was a trick question, too. If you are a Corporate Toady, you would probably answer yes. But if you are a Dot-Com Dynamo, you probably wouldn't care if the whole world, including your boss, saw you in your pajamas. Let it all hang out, baby. Let it be.

But the death of personal communications in the dot-com world is an issue that all managers, old world and new, will have to address. Because it is changing the relationships people in the workplace have with each other, and thus changing the dynamics of how things get done.

Now those of you who have been raised in the world of the Internet and the Intranet will argue that things like e-mail and voice mail are not throwing up walls, but rather empowering people to become more efficient by tearing down the physical barriers to the transfer of information.

— ◆ —

If you knew you could get through the business day without seeing anyone, wouldn't you wear pajamas to work?

— ◆ —

The ability to send text messages and documents and video and audio electronically via e-mail has saved American business time and money. Now we can talk for a moment about the fact that 90 percent of the e-mails I get are fancy graphics that fall into the "you'll never believe this" category, and raise only this issue: "If the person who created this had this much spare time on his hands, couldn't it be put to better use?"

But perhaps many of you out there consider e-mails with attachments like a video of a circus clown running headfirst into a horse's butt or a photo of the half-decomposed body of a slow-running hiker in the belly of an alligator to be examples of the high potential of the medium, and you may not like what I have to say next.

Things like e-mail and voice mail are the devil's work. Not because they aren't useful for some tasks. But because they have become ubiquitous as tools for communication between people, and even worse, tools for management of people. Like many tools, they are often used for the wrong purposes, and are abused by those who have learned to use them well.

Both e-mail and voice mail encourage selective response behavior. In other words, if you receive an e-mail you don't agree with or dislike, you don't have to return it. You can ignore it. You can say you didn't see it. No one will know. You can say, "Oh, I get a thousand e-mails a day. I must have skipped over it." You can say, "I deleted it by mistake." Or you can wait until you have found an appropriate answer or excuse before you respond. You are not on the spot. You know how sometimes you get into conversations with people, and after they are over, you think of all the great things you should have said? With e-mail or voice mail, you can take your time. Think about all those snappy comebacks before you respond. No matter what you do, you are in control.

This passive-aggressive behavior enabled by these electronic communication tools is used effectively by some managers. It is a vile way to manage, but it is becoming more common.

I had a boss who became skilled at using these devices to manipulate and manage. She demanded to be kept in the

loop of all things going on in my work world. Nothing was
too small or insignificant. It was not my job to edit, only to
inform. "I'll ignore whatever I think isn't relevant," she
would say. Sort of like the way they say the human body
disposes of excess vitamins.

Problem was, she would often ignore messages in
which I voiced an opinion or a point of view that was different from her own. She basically didn't acknowledge that
with which she did not agree. Even if I tried to slip in such

— ◆ —

I was reminded once again

of the disconnecting

power of new technology

in the hands of a madman.

— ◆ —

a message in the middle of an involved e-mail conversation—so I knew she was there at her computer, paying
attention—she would stonewall me on a distasteful subject. The fact that she ignored it sent the message that not
only was it in conflict with her view of the world, it was
also unimportant. End of dialogue.

Voice mail is also a dangerous tool of such managers.
And for those of you who work in companies that have far-
flung operations that don't or can't use an intranet system

with e-mail, you have probably been on the losing end of a voice mail management situation.

I had a boss who used voice mail to give orders and reprimands, even those of significant importance. He would go into lengthy discussions on voice mail about certain projects or issues, sometimes going on for so long that he would have to leave several messages in a row to complete his thought. It was not uncommon for me to come into work some mornings, dial up the voice mail service, and hear the voice say, "You have eleven new messages." They were all from the same person.

But if I tried the same trick, watch out. One day, in an effort to save time, and thinking that voice mail tag was his preferred method of communication, I voiced an opinion in a message back to him. "I think your memo outlining the main issues of the crisis needs some reworking. I will have a redraft with my thoughts on your desk by five."

Boy, did I get a blast. In person. Moments after I left the voice mail I was summoned to his office. There he was, behind his desk, fuming.

"This is absolutely inappropriate to send to me in voice mail."

What he was really saying was, how dare you disagree with me, in any way, in any form.

All I really noticed was that he had grown a beard since I last saw him, and I was reminded once again of the disconnecting power of new technology in the hands of a madman.

This technology has changed the way people communicate with their customers, too, and this is a serious issue in the dot-com world. In the universe of online shopping, the personal interaction between the customer and the clerk or salesperson or associate is no longer there. There is no eye contact, no body language, no feeling. "So what?" you ask. Who needs that anyway if you can get the product you want in less time at a competitive price delivered to your door without ever having to leave your house?

That is, indeed, one of the powers of the Internet. But to make such a transaction happen, no matter what you are selling, means a change in the nature of trust between people. Between customer and whoever it is on your end of the T1 line who is merchandising, processing the order, and shipping it out. It means that the customer must place his entire trust in an unseen, unknown entity, giving personal information, credit card information, preferences, shipping addresses—all kinds of stuff.

The fact that hundreds of millions of people do it every year online shows how comfortable we are becoming with the new technology. But you know what? An interesting thing happened on the way to the Internet, something all the techies failed to take into account. People like to get out from behind their computer screens and their televisions and their telephones once in a while and go outside; go to the store; and, gasp, actually pick up and touch, taste, and feel what they are buying. They like to talk to a real live human being, ask questions, ask opinions, watch their faces to see if they mean what they say or whether they are just being good salespeople.

One of the great myths of the Internet was that online shopping would kill traditional stores. That the convenience of being able to find everything online and have it delivered to your door would mean people would never have to go anywhere again. It was a dream born of the dot-com generation, but it failed to account for something that many techies don't believe in: human interaction.

The lesson here is pretty clear. Trust, whether it is between colleagues or between customer and provider, has changed. But the trust that comes from face-to-face contact will never be displaced by technology. From time to time, people want to see whom they are dealing with, they want to see a place of business, not just a Web address. It makes people feel comfortable, confident. It is human nature.

You think I'm exaggerating. Consider this. When Charles Schwab started its online brokerage firm, the concept was considered revolutionary. Anyone with a certain amount of money could open an account and trade stocks online at will. These people could do it at home, from the office, from anywhere they could get access to a computer and an Internet hookup. They didn't need a broker. That was old economy. They didn't need a face or a person. They could get all the research information they needed to make decisions from the Internet.

The predictions about how this would affect the world of Wall Street were dire for old-style firms. The conclusion: Almost overnight, all trading in stocks would be done online through some central clearinghouse technology center in Iowa. Traditional brokerage houses would die. The thousands of brokerage offices around the country with names like Merrill Lynch and PaineWebber and Prudential Securities would be boarded up. The job market would be flooded with out-of-work stockbrokers looking for new lines of work.

Then a most extraordinary thing happened. Charles Schwab started building branch offices. Not one or two. Not dozens. Hundreds. The firm now has more branch offices around the United States than many of its "old-world" rivals.

Why? The same basic principle of human nature that has foiled the Internet's promise of killing the bricks-and-mortar world. People like to be close to their stuff, in this case money. No matter how technologically savvy a person

— ◆ —

The trust that comes from face-to-face contact will never be displaced by technology.

— ◆ —

is, once in a while she likes to get up from behind her computer terminal and walk down to the local bank or brokerage office to see her money, or at least see where it is kept. It's a matter of comfort. She knows that if she ever needs that money, it's not just some blinking lights on a computer screen or a computerized voice on the bank's customer service account hotline. There is a place, with walls and doors and a big lock on it, where her pile sits. She trusts that place to keep her pile safe and secure and at her disposal when she needs it. She sleeps better at night, knowing it is so.

If you are a Corporate Toady, keep this in mind when you enter the dot-com world. Because while you will be required to adopt a lot of the communications tools in vogue today—and indeed you will be tempted to use nothing but—resist the temptation to do all of your communicating this way. Try to coax the techies out from behind their computers and their wireless devices. Help them learn to talk to you while looking you in the eye. Teach them to understand expressions on your face, body language. Salute once in a while, or use other gestures, to show them the power of the human body as a communications tool. Teach them that trust, real trust, comes from human interaction. It will help them get along better, not only with colleagues, but it will also help them understand that behind those e-mails, customers are flesh and blood too. They have hopes and dreams and aspirations. And they have fears. Anything and everything you can do to understand and empathize with them will improve the level of trust on both sides of the computer screen, and the ease with which it flows to and fro.

If you are a Dot-Com Dynamo, pay close attention to this. Be aware that there is life beyond the computer screen. Don't let all these cool devices become crutches instead of useful tools of the trade. No matter how much you liked the movie *Demon Seed*, remember that it was only a movie, dammit. And a creepy one at that. I mean, do you really think that Julie Christie was actually impregnated by a machine? And that she had its baby? You really have to stop chewing on used AAA batteries while you're reading that e-book in bed at night.

So here's a little advice. The next time you have a great idea, call someone up and talk about it. If you get their voice mail, don't leave a message. Get up from your desk and walk over to their office. Too scary? O.K., we'll start with something a little more modest, a little less intimidating. The next time you go to a CyberCafé, leave your laptop closed and talk directly to someone at the next table. They might be weirded out, but they'll be curious. "What is this," they will mutter, "this new, peculiar form of communication?" It was the same reaction the white settlers had when they first saw smoke signals. Very cool, very new. Even though it was countless centuries old.

chapter fourteen

On Entitlement

R emember phrases like "Confidential"? "Need to Know"? For Your Eyes Only"? If you do, you are so old economy. You probably obeyed the note on the gift under the tree that said "Do not open till Xmas." Sucker. You've got a lot to learn in the dot-com world.

Because, you see, that kind of exclusionary jargon just doesn't fly in a world where everything, including information, is democratized. You can't keep people out. You can't leave them in the dark. Like the song says:

Sign, sign,
Everywhere a sign.

How did it go?

Do this, don't do that,
Can't you read the sign?

(And if you remember that song, and liked it, you're just an old rebel yourself.)

Indeed, the old notion of entitlement, which had become restricted to the chosen few in the old economy, has found new, much broader life in the dot-com world. Entitlement isn't something granted to you based on your

— ◆ —

But this was dot-com,

where the peasants

run the palace.

— ◆ —

relative loftiness on the corporate totem; it is a God-given right. It doesn't matter what your position or tenure in the company is, you have the right to know everything there is to know about what's going on in the company, and to use that information in any way you see fit. The idea of earning privilege and access is positively ancient, a vestige of monarchies and their crazy monarchs.

Consider this. A friend of mine, the CEO of a dot-com company, was pleased that despite difficult times, the company would have a holiday party for its employees. It would not be the lavish event of the past, but a more modest offering with some food, beer, and wine, and with a disc jockey instead of a live band. A nice gesture. And an important gesture, from a morale-building point of view for loyal employees.

He called me one day, not long after the party, with a problem. It seems that one of the freelance consultants who worked for the company was complaining about not having been invited to the party.

"She has sent me ten e-mails complaining. I tried to explain that it's for employees only. That's the policy for all these kinds of events."

I failed to see how this was a problem. It was more of an annoyance. I also thought it was a little ballsy of a part-time contract worker to be busting the CEO's chops over a holiday party. I mean, if I were going to raise a stink about something with the head of the company, it would be for something more important than a chance to eat some stale cold cuts and sing karaoke. If I were not an employee, I'd think more than twice before complaining about having access to something that was clearly out of my sphere. But this was dot-com, where the peasants run the palace.

"Now, I'm starting to get complaints from employees," the CEO said. "They don't like the way she's being treated. I've tried to explain that the reason we call it an "employee party" is because it's for employees. Outside consultants who work part time on a contract basis are not employees."

The goal at this point was to defuse the crisis. Worry about the fairness and appropriateness of the policy later. If it were perceived to be unfair, no rationalization would change that perception. I asked if there were any other events coming up where the inclusion of part-time workers might be appropriate. Where he could, by invitation, extend an olive branch.

The CEO thought for a minute. Yes, there was a casual holiday lunch, to be served in the office, to thank those people who had to work over the holidays. "I will invite her to that," he said, quite pleased with himself.

Not long after the scheduled lunch, I called him to see whether the crisis had been averted.

"I'm glad you called," he said, sounding rather glum. "I'm reading an e-mail from our part-time complainer. She's still complaining. This time about the food at the lunch. She suggested we have turkey next year. More appropriate for the season, she says. You just can't win, can you?"

No you can't. In a world where everyone feels entitled, it's hard to do anything right if you're a manager. This attitude can be more than an annoyance, too, because it makes it very difficult to control messages inside and outside the company. Imposing rules and regulations and processes is not an easy task because these things, by nature, restrict the access certain people have to certain things. They need to, because not everyone needs to know everything that goes on in the company.

Let's face it, if everyone from top to bottom knew everything about your company's development efforts, your financial details, your competitive plans, you'd be sunk. Because in the era of the Internet, that stuff would be circulated in a heartbeat to everyone, everywhere.

Indeed, it is this sense of entitlement at all levels of a dot-com that makes managing and controlling a company's public profile very difficult. Everyone thinks they are empowered to speak about what's going on in the company. To their friends. To their colleagues. To the news media. They feel they should be well enough informed to speak on behalf of the company to anyone who will listen. And sometimes, they do.

It's not like the old economy at all. Back then, we had strict policies that said only certain people were allowed to talk to outside parties about the company. Indeed, any incoming calls from reporters or investment analysts or shareholders had to be directed to the appropriate department for response. Failure to do so—or worse, participation in unauthorized interviews, even if they consisted simply of a "no comment"—were firing offenses. There was no argument. The only way to present a consistent, professional face to the outside world was to have a single, centralized gatekeeper of the company line.

Those of you who are still wondering why a "no comment" could get you fired need to know this. If you are asked by a reporter or an investment analyst why the company is spending $50 million on a new warehouse, and you say "no comment," you have responded as an official spokesperson of the company. What if the company wants to talk about the warehouse? Wants to explain to those important audiences like the news media and Wall Street that despite the expenditure, the cost savings and improved customer service over time as the business achieves scale will put the company in a much better situation financially and competitively. What if this is something that the chairman himself has decided is an important enough issue for the company that he wants to talk about it and, indeed, already has participated in a lengthy interview set to be released in next week's *Fortune*. And you said "no comment."

You see, you don't know everything. And you don't need to know everything. That's why people have different, distinct, and separate jobs in companies. It's not anti-teamwork. It's pro-judgment. When you've been around long enough, you'll understand this better.

It's a particularly important point for companies that are publicly traded, or those that are considering such a move. During the IPO bonanza of the late 1990s, dot-com companies went from conception to inception to publicly traded

—◆—

In the 1960s, it was love

that was free; in dot-com,

it was data.

—◆—

entities in a matter of months. Who cared what anyone said to the press or the Street as long as the Web site was cool and the beer was cold? So anyone who felt like it said anything they wanted to say. And it was reported as gospel.

Oh, and this brings me to the subject of conferences. One of the great boondoggles of the dot-com world. Where else would 500 people fly thousands of miles or more to hear a twenty-three-year-old direct marketing whiz deliver the keynote address? And think they were actually getting something out of it? And what company would trust such a person to know what to say, especially if asked tough questions?

But again, this practice became almost second nature, because in the Internet space, the democratization of information meant it was for everyone to know, everyone to consume, and everyone to deliver. There were no secrets in the Internet world. In the 1960s, it was love that was free; in dot-com, it was data. And it was dispensed and devoured by the datadumpful.

Perpetuating this activity has been the human resources argument that in a competitive job market, entitlement and access are definite lures in the recruitment and training of good talent. The logic goes something like this: You have to tell employees everything or they will get mad at you. And if they get mad at you, they will leave. And in the early days of the Internet, they could. Now the reality of the market has limited that somewhat.

Still, the sense of entitlement lives on. And it is something that you must face head-on if you are a traditionally trained manager. Corporate Toadies will have a difficult time with this, simply because they are not used to knowing everything themselves. If you're a Corporate Toady, you have been weaned on a system in which selective disclosure is the norm, not the exception. Information was doled out to you in bits, sort of like you were on a spy mission. If you knew how to build the entire bomb, and not just the little piece you were working on, you would be dangerous. They would have to kill you. And they would. This is not a bad thing to remember, and take with you to the dot-com. A little fear is a great lever for managers.

Problem is, in a world where such secrecy doesn't exist, the plans for the bomb are not only sitting on the cafeteria table, where people can absorb them while they eat lunch, they are also being circulated by e-mail throughout cyberspace, where everyone can see them.

Now, it's your butt on the line to keep those plans safe. What do you do? Well, first, you take the plans out of the cafeteria. Next, you kill the e-mail. (It may be too late, but at least it sends another, different message that such dissemination will not be tolerated.) Then, you lock the plans

— ◆ —

In a world where secrecy doesn't exist, the plans for the bomb are sitting on the cafeteria table.

— ◆ —

in your desk, and if an underling demands to see them, you simply say they are on a confidential, need-to-know, my-eyes-only basis. None of your beeswax. And if they get mad, too bad. Welcome to the real world where the grown-ups hold the key to the cookie cupboard.

If you're a Closet Creative, you may have a little more trouble holding this hard line because, in a way, you too think you should be entitled to see more than you've ever been shown before. This democratization of information isn't such a bad thing, after all. You're mature. You're responsible. After all, when your dad let you use the car in high school, you brought it back without a scratch. You didn't notice that he was following you around all night in your mom's car, just to make sure.

You Desperately Seeking Somethings should take this very valuable lesson with you before you jump into the dot-com world, especially now. It's not the free-for-all it was a year or two ago. You really have to pay attention to what you're supposed to do, rather than what everyone else is doing. As they used to say, pay attention to the nickels, and the dollars will take care of themselves. Or some old-economy expression.

Same goes for Dot-Com Dynamos. The "new" new economy will require a concentration and dedication to the task at hand that has not yet been seen in Internet space. There will be a premium on talented people who can focus on their jobs, do them well, excel. It is not simply an objective for which to strive. It is all about survival.

Over time, if you do the old-economy nose-to-the-grindstone shtick, the entitlement will come to you. You will get to see more and more of the plans. You will be included more often and in greater context in important strategic and development initiatives. You will have your own kick at developing policy. But in the meantime, be patient, be cool. And remember, some things simply aren't your business. Yet.

chapter fifteen

On the Future

At the height of the Internet consolidation in 2000, the news media was full of stories about the broken dreams of twenty-something workers who got gypped out of their instant millions when the market woke up and realized that this thing called dot-com was a business, not a day at the beach, and that a lot of companies in the dot-com space were masquerading as legitimate entities.

It was sad, really, reading about the twenty-seven-year-old former dot-com senior vice president who was out on the street, worried that he would have to take a lower-level job at a, gulp, traditional company. That all he had to show for his fifteen minutes as a senior executive at a dot-com company was a handful of worthless stock options and a T-shirt that said "Web Genius."

Secretly, of course, many millions of traditional managers were cheering. It was no longer revenge of the nerds, but revenge of the suits. These young know-it-alls had finally gotten their comeuppance.

I was at a breakfast with a bunch of blue-suited accountants the day that yet another dot-com went under, and the speaker, an economist, said something about the swift and stinging justice of the marketplace, the bursting of the balloon, and the era of the deflated ego. How he couldn't wait

— ◆ —

All he had to show for his fifteen minutes as a senior executive at a dot-com was a handful of worthless stock options and a T-shirt that said "Web Genius."

— ◆ —

until the next ex-dot-comer came into his office, looking for a job, so that he could make the kid grovel. Remind him that the excesses of dot-com were all a dream. Welcome to reality, kid. And people applauded. Some even let out a little cheer. "It's about time," they muttered.

And despite their elation that reality had cut the dot-com generation down to size, they didn't realize that at the same time they had inherited a big problem. And it had to do with the future. Or more precisely, the difference between their concept of the future and that of the Interneters who were now flooding the marketplace.

Because one of the big lessons of the dot-com world for managers of all stripes is that the future of business really has changed because of the Internet. We all knew that time had been compressed because of the technology's power and influence. But all the cultural changes that were occurring as the dot-com world went through its development have had an equally profound impact on how people view the future, or need to view the future. So all you old-economy managers out there who are still snickering with delight about the blip in the dot-com development curve that brought so many crashing back down to earth, stop laughing. The reality is just as real for you.

Because in the dot-com world, the future is something that is only a few months, or perhaps a few years, long. That's why stock options with a vesting period of several years were hard for people to comprehend. That kind of timeline made sense in the old economy, but to a twenty-five-year-old, four years from now is an eternity.

There are side effects to this short horizon. Dot-comers are easily disillusioned by things that don't go their way. When the concept of commerce impedes their objective of doing something cool. Or watching a project or a company fail. It is easy to lose focus when your view of the world is only a few months long.

Like novice investors in the stock market, dot-comers have been easily spooked by bumps in the road. They had never seen the Internet version of a bear market, a downturn, a correction. And when it came, it was devastating.

Of course, this behavior is easily explained. It is a function of inexperience, and of the kind of irrational exuberance that comes from being involved in a business that in its early days grew and grew and grew to heights that even the most seasoned veterans of business had never even imagined. This rocket in the Internet world created ridiculous expectations in every way. From compensation, to responsibility, to success, to retirement—and all on a condensed time line. The people who entered the dot-com world in its early days didn't think about thirty-year careers. They thought about quick scores. In and out in five years, max. And it really had very little to do with age or the generation gap. If they were twenty-five, retirement was a real possibility at thirty. If they were forty-five, it was fifty. Time and the future changed forever.

And traditional managers have to understand and adapt. Sure, there is still a place for the old economy's long-term view. Like investors, you should be in a job or the stock market for the long term. Don't get flustered by the ups and downs. Don't watch the ticker. Fluctuations are all part of the business cycle. Like your personal life. Every day isn't a great day. Some are better than others. You win some, you lose some. But over time, if you average out on the plus side, you manage.

This long-term view helps focus, too. If you're not fretting and jumping up and down about the bumps in the road, you are more likely able to pay attention to your big goals, big objectives. The big idea behind your career and your life. You are not spooked by rapid change or unexpected hurdles thrown up in your path.

These attributes come through only one thing: experience. Even knowledge alone won't get you there. You have to live it. As they say about commentators in sports, until you've crossed the white line onto the playing field, you really have no idea what it's all about. You can only speculate. Experience gives you perspective, understanding. It turns knowledge into wisdom.

— ◆ —

You will realize that hierarchy for hierarchy's sake is as ridiculous a concept as a nap room.

— ◆ —

Somewhere between the youthful, shortsighted exuberance of the early Internet and the wizened been-there, done-that of the old economy lies the attitude of the next generation of dot-com. Somewhere between "anything's possible" and "let's see whether we can make it last." Somewhere between yes and no lies maybe so.

How do we get there? Well, it will be a bit of a struggle. We have all of these very talented, very enthusiastic, though somewhat disillusioned, dot-comers who are looking for jobs. For a while, they can hold on to their unrealistic expectations. But when the rent is past due and Napster eventually becomes a pay-to-use service, which it will, reality will set in and companies, old economy and new, will benefit.

These people, like the companies that survive and prosper in the dot-com world, will have learned an important
lesson: that this is a business, not a game. And if you lose,
you can't simply push the reset button and play again.

But if you've been paying attention, you will realize that
there is a lot to be learned from the dot-com experience.
That a shorter-term view of the world is not necessarily a
bad thing, in certain circumstances. That a lack of process
can actually be a benefit, such as moving ideas from concept to market in a fraction of the time. That hierarchy for

— ◆ —

It's like having a Ph.D.

in idea generation, in thinking fast

on your feet, in being fearless.

— ◆ —

hierarchy's sake is as ridiculous a concept as a nap room.
That it isn't the clothes that make the man or the woman.
It's the ideas, the willingness to listen and learn. To focus
on what's best for the company, not what's best for yourself.
After all, that's why they call it work, and not play. This sort
of stuff can be a big competitive benefit to companies, old
and new.

Managers of all stripes, but especially you Corporate
Toadies, need to pay attention. Take a lesson from the
Closet Creatives. Loosen up a little. Open your mind.

There is more than one good way to do something. And more to the point, there may be a much better way to do something than the way you've been using.

Closet Creatives, keep doing what you're doing, only more so. Take with you to the dot-com world the sense of purpose and common sense and respect for responsibility and accountability that you have learned in the old economy. But continue to step out, embrace those new ideas, those new ways of doing things. Keep experimenting, keep trying new things. You are already predisposed to have an open mind. Don't lose that ability. It will make you a great dot-comer.

Desperately Seeking Somethings may have the most difficult time of all adjusting. You have not been through the early wars of the Internet. You have not experienced the highs and lows of a young, growing business. You have not been humbled by the realities of the marketplace. You cling to your ideals, your lofty expectations. Take stock of the situation. Talk to your friends. Do your homework. You will need to have a lot more than dreams to make it here.

As for the Dot-Com Dynamos, don't despair. You really are pioneers. And like any person or group that breaks new ground, some people will always think you're crazy. Look at the great explorers of civilization. The Vikings. Christopher Columbus. Lewis and Clark. People thought they were nuts for risking their lives in the unknown. Until, of course, they returned home with untold riches, tangible and intangible.

The experience you have gained, albeit limited, when combined with your strong sense of boldly going where no one has gone before, is the kind of combination that is the foundation of great future managers. You have proved yourself. Now take the time to study the realities of the new landscape. Take what you know and adapt them. Be patient. Listen to those suits. They're the ones who can help create value for your company, and for yourself.

Whatever you do, don't lose the dot-com outlook. It's like having a Ph.D. in idea generation, in thinking fast on your feet, in being fearless. It is at the heart of every great entrepreneur in the history of the business world. And it will be the foundation of the next generation of Internet companies.

Conclusion

Are you ready? Do you feel it? Do you feel lucky? Do you?

Do you dot-com?

If you're still a little skeptical, don't feel too bad. I've been doing it for almost two years and I'm still terrified every morning when I go to work. Terrified that no matter how hard I try to keep up, I am still a step behind. Maybe more. And that I will never, ever close the gap completely.

But look at it this way. Don't you think the farmers who went into those first factories of the Industrial Revolution felt a little trepidation? Don't you think they were dazed and confused by the noise and the smell and power of the machines? I mean, these guys were used to wide open spaces, the phases of the moon, the vagaries of nature, the power that a couple of horses could generate. Don't you think they had a tough time adjusting to working inside, confined by four walls, in artificially timed shifts, in a new, horrifying environment around man-made monsters that could crush a man like a bug?

Of course they were scared. Change is a frightening thing. It is upsetting, discombobulating, to use a scientific term. But it can also be stimulating, exciting.

— ◆ —

One of the defining characteristics of the dot-com world is that it defies definition.

— ◆ —

There is no question that the dot-com world is all those things, and more. It is young, it is headstrong. It has an energy like nothing else. And when you combine that much energy with that much youth, and stir in a healthy dose of inexperience, you have a powder keg. It blows up every day, in a different way. But everyone just puts out the fires and moves on.

If you want to dot-com, the best advice I can give you is to leave all your preconceived notions of what work should be at the door. It doesn't matter whether those notions are the products of a long career as a Corporate Toady, the longings of a Closet Creative, the aspirations of a Desperately Seeking Something, or the tragically hip experience of a Dot-Com Dynamo. No matter what corner you're coming from, be prepared to look at new ways to do things, new concepts of time, space, and what's important. Because if you try to fit the dot-com world into your own personal box, no matter what box that may be, you'll fail. Even worse, you'll be unhappy. Just remember that one of the defining characteristics of the dot-com world is that it defies definition.

But don't leave everything you've learned behind. No matter what your age or experience, bring your common sense. The rules of reasonableness haven't changed, only the tools we use to apply them. If you remember that, you won't just succeed, you'll have some fun, too.

So think about it. If any of the issues I raised here sound like serious trouble for you, take a pass. The last thing you want to do is follow the hype into an unhappy situation.

But if all this crazy stuff that goes on in Internet companies doesn't faze you—or better yet, if it gets you jazzed up—go ahead. Do the dot-com. And forget about the fact that you may look funny doing it. Everyone does. That's what it's all about.

Index